THE TRUTH WILL SET US FREE

ARMENIANS AND TURKS RECONCILED

GEORGE JERJIAN

Published by GJ Communications, London UK (2003)

For orders
Email: georgejerjian@btinternet.com
Telephone: +44 (0)20 7823 6349
Fax: +44 (0)20 7823 6348

Front cover photo by Dan Stevens, Woodstock Studios, London

Designed and typeset by Sue Lamble, London
Printed and bound by Biddles Ltd of King's Lynn

Copyright © George Jerjian, April 2002

All rights reserved. No part of this publication may be reproduced, stored in a retrieval system, or transmitted, in any form or by any means without the prior written permission of the author, nor be otherwise circulated in any form or binding or cover other than that in which it is being published and without a similar condition being imposed on the subsequent purchaser.

George Jerjian has asserted his right under the UK Copyright, Designs and Patents Act 1988, to be identified as the author of this work.

This title is registered with the United States Copyright Office Certificate # TXu 1-046-836 on 6 June, 2002

ISBN: 0-9544599-0-3

A CIP catalogue record for this book is available from the British Library (UK)

Publisher's Cataloging in Publication
(Provided by Quality Books, Inc.)
Jerjian, George.
 The truth will set us free: Armenians and Turks reconciled / George Jerjian.
 p. cm.
 ISBN 0-9544599-0-3

 1. Armenian question. 2. Armenians—Turkey—History.
 3. Genocide—Turkey. 4. Turkey—History—20th century
 5. Armenia—History—1901– I. Title.

 DS195.J47 2003   956.6´2
                          QB133–1526

"There are few higher callings than exposing historic lies that stifle personal liberty and economic progress. Jerjian rises to the task, exposing the truth and discovering painful truths about his own family's past. In this eloquently written and powerfully argued book, he shows that the simple and plain truth is neither simple nor plain. Read this book if you want to understand why progress is a mirage in this part of the world."
   Hirair Hovnanian, Chairman, Armenian Assembly of America, Washington DC

"George Jerjian not only gives the readers a meaningful insight into one of most troubling episodes of the grim history of the 20th century, but also builds up a challenging and optimistic scenario regarding the future of the region. Reading Jerjian's admirable book one is reminded of a quote from Herman Kahn, the founding father of scenario methodology, who once noted: "History is likely to write scenarios that most observers would find implausible not only prospectively, but sometimes, even in retrospect. Many sequences of events seem plausible now only because they have actually occurred; a man who knew no history might not believe any. Future events may not be drawn from a restricted list of those we have learned are possible; we should expect to go on being surprised." As Jerjian amply illustrates, the bleak history of the region in the 20th century surprised us with its brutality too many times. One can only hope that the 21st century history of the region will surprise us in a positive way confirming Jerjian's optimistic scenario. Jerjian's work is to be applauded."

Paul Dragos Aligica, Fellow, the Hudson Institute, US Think Tank, Indianapolis

"Jerjian has given us a heartfelt and effective statement for the case for bringing Armenians and Turks to a kind of reconciliation on the troubled issue of the Genocide of 1915. In his rendering of historical accounts and plea for understanding, the author is able to separate the horrors of distant events from present-day hopes for a different relationship between two peoples whose fate and future are permanently linked."

Professor Ronald G Suny, Department of Political Science, The University of Chicago

"George Jerjian's *The Truth Will Set Us Free* is a lucid, factual, and necessary primer on the Armenian genocide. He not only tells us the terrible story but he also gives a balanced view of Turkey's position on the affair and presents a plan to help Turks and Armenians reconcile, however difficult such a step seems. The booklet should be read in every high school and studied and carried by every lawmaker."

Michael Chapman, Editorial Director,
Cato Institute, Washington DC

"George Jerjian's book promotes a vision that leads toward recognition by Turkey in 2015 of the Armenian Genocide of 1915. In so doing, it fosters reconciliation based on truth. It also charts the way forward so that Armenians and Turks can find closure to an ongoing denial of historical truth and can then proceed to live as neighbors of a global village in harmony, justice and mutual respect. For all readers interested in the integrity of a vision that feels the deep pain associated with the Armenian Genocide, Jerjian's book is a 'must read' as it unpacks the stories of the past, comments on the issues of the present and offers hope for the future.

Dr Rostom Stepanian, MD, FRCP
Chair, Campaign for Recognition of the Armenian
Genocide, London

"George Jerjian has found a persuasive and engaging combination in *The Truth Will Set Us Free*. Against the backdrop of a lively retelling of his own family's experience of the time, his ability to compress historical detail clarifies the legal case for recognizing the Armenian genocide. Most importantly, he is brave enough to imagine a way forward post-recognition, where Turks and Armenians are reconciled and working together to help re-create a new, much-improved version of the old Near eastern mosaic. Jerjian must be congratulated for daring to dream and for having the courage to stir debate in the public forum."

Dr Susan Pattie, Senior Research Fellow (Anthropology), University College London

"In recounting his family's survival of the Armenian genocide and the compelling arguments for recognition, George Jerjian provides a fascinating proposal for reconciliation between Armenians and Turks that will spawn justice to the peoples of both lands."

Dr Levon Chorbajian, Professor of Sociology, University of Massachusetts Lowell

Whatever our nationality, we all carry some horrors in our historical baggage. My country Britain was, for example, a leader in the slave trade. As George Jerjian says in this timely book, only by facing up to the past and laying to rest its ghosts can we build a future together in peace, prosperity and confidence, with that enjoyment of unity in diversity, which is the embodiment of the European dream.

Baroness Sarah Ludford MEP

To Talyn, for enduring the "truth" with a smile

Contents

Foreword *Former Senator Bob Dole*	x
Acknowledgments	xii
Preface	xiv
Prologue *The story of Cain and Abel*	1
PART I ◆ *The Past*	
The honorable Turk: Nonna's story	4
PART II ◆ *The Present*	
Protecting the truth	33
PART III ◆ *The Future*	
I have a dream	68
Appendices	92

Foreword

In the spring of 1945, while serving in the US Army in Italy, I was hit by Nazi machine gun fire. I survived with a shattered right shoulder and paralyzed from the neck down. It took nearly three years and many operations to take care of all my problems. In these trying years, the people of Russell, Kansas my hometown, stood by me both financially and spiritually and I never forgot what that help meant.

Then I met Hampar Kelikian – Dr K to his friends. An Armenian immigrant, who lost his family in the 1915 genocide, Kelikian was a pioneer in the surgical restoration of otherwise useless limbs. Dr K was frank to say that after that, it would be up to me to make the most of what I had. There would be no miracles, he added. But he was wrong. Dr K himself was a miracle. He would not take a penny for any of the operations and did the same for many young veterans coming back from the war who could not afford the medical care they needed. So, you can imagine how I cherished the friendship of Dr Kelikian.

I know Dr K would have been proud of George Jerjian's splendid book *The Truth Will Set Us Free: Armenians and Turks Reconciled,* because like him, George is also a pioneer; a pioneer in the complex restoration of relations between the Armenians and Turks.

Former Senator Bob Dole
Washington DC, March 2003

Acknowledgements

I thank my wife, Talyn, for her help and support on this book from inception to completion and especially during the trying times when I almost gave up on this project.

I thank my daughters, Victoria and Elizabeth, for their spirited encouragement. I thank my mother, Molly, for her insights, her memories and her reasoned judgments.

I thank my editors, Amanda Gray and Daniel Hahn; book designer Sue Lamble; and everyone at Biddles Ltd who was involved in publishing this book.

My special thanks to all those people who read the book and gave me their feedback, which helped me to improve and sharpen it – especially Archbishop Yeghishe Gizirian, Professor Vahakn Dadrian, Dr Susan Pattie, Arda Kassabian, John B Kurkjian, Paul Kassabian, and Dr Harry Hagopian.

My gratitude to those people who helped to promote the book, especially Chris Jerjian, Avo Izmirlian, Dickran Izmirlian, and Michael and Phillipa Harrison.

Last, but not least, I make grateful acknowledgment to the following for using in whole or in part previously published material: Turkish Odyssey, Turkish Ministry of Foreign Affairs, Groong, Zoryan Institute, Le Monde Diplomatique, Media Monitors Network, World Policy Journal, New Perspectives Quarterly, Armenian National Institute and Editions Autrement.

Preface

The purpose of this book is to share three separate, but inter-linked stories with Armenians, Turks and other nations, who share an interest in the resolution of the Armenian genocide and reconciliation between Armenians and Turks. The book is divided into three parts, all of which can stand on their own, but together form a journey of honor, truth and hope.

Part I is about duty to country and honor to friends. In it, I narrate my grandmother's story, in which an "honorable" Turk saves her and her family. Although I did not know at the time I started this book or even when I had finished writing the first draft, I discovered from the acclaimed genocide scholar, Professor Vahakn Dadrian, that this Turk was listed in the British Foreign Office archives as one of 144 high-ranking Ottoman officials responsible for the annihilation of Armenians. You will discover that the simple and plain truth is neither simple nor plain.

Preface

Part II is about truth. Truth is agreement with reality. Truth is being accurate, genuine and honest. Truth is not negotiable. In it, I share the compelling evidence of an Armenian professor, who unearths new and very credible evidence of Armenocide by Ottoman Turkey. I share the findings of a Turkish scholar, who implicates the Turkish Republic in covering up this genocide and an American journalist, a Turcophile, who reveals why he believes the Turks are stuck in a time warp, from which they are unable to emerge.

Part III is about hope. In it, I create a vision of the future, of possibilities, of opportunities. This vision is entirely mine and it is fluid and not written in stone. It does not represent the vision of the Armenian Republic nor of any Armenian Diaspora institution or groups. It is simply meant to start a conversation among and between Armenians and Turks. A note of caution to our fellow compatriots, our friends in the legislatures of the United States and the European Union and to our Turkish detractors, this book is not a call for disengagement from the issue of recognition of the Armenian genocide. On the contrary, it is a call to double our efforts in order to reach a goal, which is recognition and then reconciliation.

The Turkish Armenian Reconciliation Commission (TARC), formed in July 2001 by Turkish and Armenian civil society representatives, requested the International Center for Transitional Justice (ICTJ) to facilitate an independent legal study on whether the 1948 Genocide Convention applied to the events in Eastern Anatolia in 1915. On 4 February 2003, ICTJ declared, "The events, viewed collectively, can be said to include all of the elements of the crime of genocide as defined in the Convention, and legal scholars as well as historians, politicians, journalists and other people would be justified in continuing to so describe them."

Will this be enough to reach reconciliation? No. Armenians will need to overcome their high expectations of what Turkish recognition of the genocide will mean and in turn, the Turks will need to overcome the serious limitations of their high school history syllabus. Reconciliation can only take place when truth and truce are declared. What happened cannot be undone, but we need not be prisoners of the past. The truth will set us – Armenian and Turk – free.

Lastly, it shows that while the truth is not negotiable, the terms of reconciliation are.

Turks and Armenians need a new vision; a new vision to demolish the wall; a new vision for a new century.

G E J
London, June 2003

The story of Cain and Abel

(This story is found not only in The Old Testament book of Genesis, chapter 4, but also in the Koran, "The Dinner Table", verses 5:27–5:32.)

Now Adam had marital relations with his wife Eve, and she became pregnant and gave birth to Cain. Then she said, "I have created a man just as the LORD did!" Then she gave birth to his brother Abel. Abel took care of the flocks, while Cain cultivated the ground.

At the designated time, Cain brought some of the fruit of the ground for an offering to the Lord. But Abel brought some of the firstborn of his flock – even the fattest of them. And the Lord was pleased with Abel and his offering, but with Cain and his offering he was not pleased. So Cain became very angry, and his expression was downcast.

Then the Lord said to Cain, "Why are you angry,

and why is your expression downcast? Is it not true that if you do what is right, you will be fine? But if you do not do what is right, sin is crouching at the door. It desires to dominate you, but you must suppress it."

Cain said to his brother Abel, "Let's go out to the field." While they were in the field, Cain attacked his brother Abel and killed him.

Then the Lord said to Cain, "Where is your brother Abel?" And he replied, "I don't know! Am I my brother's guardian?" But the Lord said, "What have you done? The voice of your brother's blood is crying out to me from the ground! So now, you are banished from the ground, which has opened its mouth to receive your brother's blood from your hand. When you try to cultivate the ground it will no longer yield its best for you. You will be a homeless wanderer on the earth."

Then Cain said to the Lord, "My punishment is too great to endure! Look! You are driving me off the land today and I must hide from your presence. I will be a homeless wanderer on the earth; whoever finds me will kill me." But the Lord said to him, "All right then, if anyone kills Cain, Cain will be avenged seven times as much." Then the Lord put a special mark on Cain so that no one who found him would strike him down. So Cain went out from the presence of the Lord and lived in the land of Nod, east of Eden.

PART I ◆ *The Past*

The honorable Turk: Nonna's story

Valetta, Malta, August 1920. The First World War is over and the Allied Powers have won. The Treaty of Sèvres, imposed upon the defeated Ottoman Empire, required the Ottoman government to hand over to the Allied Powers people accused of Armenian "massacres". Subsequently, 144 high-ranking Ottoman officials were arrested and deported for trial by the British to the island of Malta. Among those 144 officials was a man named Suleiman Nedjmi Bey. The British archives show him as Prisoner Number 2812, interned in Malta on 29 August 1920. It also shows him to have been the District Governor (*Mutessarif*) of Samsun, a city on the Black Sea from 1914 to 1916 and Governor (*Vali*) of Sivas province from 1916 to 1918 – see Appendix A at the end of the book.

The accusations heaped against Nedjmi Bey

came from three sources. First, there is a signed statement from a large number of Armenians from Samsun dated 1 July 1919 accusing him specifically of murdering Father Karekin Chinikjian, their local priest and Hampar Zakarian, a poor Armenian, whom he ordered stripped and tortured with red-hot irons.

They also state that Nedjmi Bey declared that any Armenians who converted to Islam would be saved, as a result of which some 300 Armenians converted, but he subsequently sent them all to Sivas, a neighboring town, into the hands of Muammer Bey, who had them massacred by organized troops. During the deportations of Armenians from Samsun, Nedjmi Bey spared no one – not even pregnant women, the sick or the priests.

The second accusation is provided by Krikor Nishanian of Trebizond, who lived in Samsun and had converted to Islam. He confirms the barbaric torture of his friend, Hampar Zakarian and the murder of Father Karekin. He also declares that another friend, Bedros Tatarian who was in hiding with his family had asked him to intercede with Nedjmi Bey to discover if they too could convert to Islam. After having agreed to his request, Nedjmi Bey then issued instructions for their arrest and immediate deportation.

Lastly, there is an extensive statement by a Hagop Guevchenian dated 5 August on the general responsibility of Nedjmi Bey for the Armenian deportations and massacres.

Nedjmi Bey was never tried or sentenced. The Malta tribunals never took place. The British camp in Malta was strictly a detention center where Turkish suspects were being held for future prosecution on charges of crimes perpetrated against Armenians. With their eye on stealing an advantage over each other, the victorious Allies struck separate deals with the rising insurgents in Anatolia led by Mustapha Kemal. In one such deal some British hostages held by Kemalists were exchanged for the liberation of the Malta detainees. In the words of British Foreign Minister Lord Curzon, "The less we say about these people [the detainees], the better... The staunch belief among Members of Parliament is that one British prisoner is worth a shipload of Turks."

Turkish records show Nedjmi Bey's full official name as Süleyman Necmi Selmen, a Circassian by origin. He was born in 1871 in a town called

The honorable Turk: Nonna's story

Bafra, near Samsun. After returning from Malta, Nedjmi Bey joined Atatürk's Anatolian uprising and was rewarded with the post of Governor of Trabzon in 1919 and Deputy Governor of Sinop and Kastamonu in 1922. After the creation of the Turkish Republic in 1923, he was elected and served for many years as congressman to Parliament representing the Samsun district. He died in 1943 quietly in his bed.[1]

The simple and plain truth is neither simple nor plain. The British Archives show Nedjmi Bey to have been, by all measures, a mass murderer, an evil monster, a twisted human being. Yet as much as I would like to hate this man, I cannot bring myself to do that. One act that this man did redeems him in my eyes: that one act is Nonna's story. Therein lies for me the paradox; a paradox I was unaware of until I started the journey of writing this book.

Khartoum, Sudan, December 1966. The BOAC VC10 aircraft banked steeply over a sand-colored, but familiar Khartoum, before landing gracefully at the airport. I emerged, welcomed first by a blast of hot and clammy Sudanese air that smacked me in the face and then by my parents, who helped to speed me through passport control and customs. I was finally home for Christmas. It was great. I would be here for a whole month, before returning to my boarding school in England. I did this journey with my three younger brothers three times a year: Christmas break, Easter break and the summer months.

My father was busy managing a successful import/export business. My mother juggled domestic affairs, her four sons and a busy social life. Only my maternal grandmother was available for us. We knew her as Nonna or "granny" in Italian: to avoid confusion with our paternal grandmother. Her real name was Victoria Kassabian and her maiden name was Tchorbajian. Nonna had plenty of time and was available at our beck and call. She lived upstairs, one floor above our apartment and she came down to spend the mornings and afternoons with us. She was a private individual, but she needed human contact.

Nonna had time for me. She listened to my stories, my feelings and my thoughts. She would make me feel important. My thoughts and feelings mattered to her. I had time for this woman. So, when she told me stories, I listened, because they drew me into her world. Her

The honorable Turk: Nonna's story

stories ranged from socially important material laced with juicy gossip of the leading families in Khartoum to stories of the experiences of the amusing and sublime Nasreddin Hodja to stories of catastrophic events that robbed her of family, home and youth. This last one was Nonna's story.

Anatolia covers the area that is known today as Asiatic Turkey. Eastern Anatolia was the heartland and homeland of Armenians for nearly 3,000 years. Armenia once had an empire that stretched from the Caspian Sea to the Mediterranean. In the last millennium, it formed part of the Ottoman Empire, ruled by Muslim Sultans in Constantinople. Armenians managed to contribute to this Empire for centuries, until such time as it became bloody, corrupt and despotic. As the First World War broke out in 1914, the Ottomans made an alliance with Imperial Germany and the Austro-Hungarian Empire against England, France and Russia. Naturally, Armenians living in the Russian sphere of influence sided with the Russians. The Ottomans feared that their Christian Armenian subjects would side with their Russian co-religionists. With their Empire in Europe diminished, the Ottomans also feared

English and French designs of carving up their Empire in Arabia. Under cover of war, in April 1915, almost to the day when British troops landed on the Turkish peninsula of Gallipoli, the Ottomans decided to ethnically cleanse Anatolia of Armenians and thereby consolidate the heartland of modern Turkey.

Tokat, Anatolia. Nonna was born on July 22, 1900 in Samsun, a cosmopolitan city on the shores of the Black Sea and home of the legendary Amazonian warrior women. She was the fourth child of Hovsep and Maritza Tchorbajian. She was very fair and had ginger hair. Her personality displayed a combination of a strong will interwoven with an intuitive sensitivity. Her childhood memories were very happy, but at the tender age of 15, events would change her life forever.

Nonna's father, Hovsep Tchorbajian, was about 5 foot 10 inches tall, with a strong-looking face, crew-cut hair and an elegant and full moustache, waxed at the ends, giving him a military air. He was born to an Armenian Catholic family in Tokat; the only son among six sisters. In 1890, having become a successful textile merchant, Hovsep, at the age of 22, married Maritza, an

The honorable Turk: Nonna's story 11

Hovsep and Maritza Tchorbajian with their eldest daughter and son, Varvar and Harootyun (Samsun, Anatolia, 1912)

elegant 15-year-old girl from his hometown.

Before marrying, Hovsep had traveled to Egypt on a specific mission. One of his elderly bachelor uncles had settled in Egypt and had died leaving a substantial fortune to his brothers. As his elderly bachelor uncles were too old to travel, they asked their nephew Hovsep to go to Egypt on their behalf, deal with the estate and return with the fortune. When he arrived in Egypt, he was obliged to stay for six months, because a distant cousin was contesting the estate. But he succeeded in proving that his uncles were the brothers of the deceased and on his return to Tokat, he gave his uncles their share and they in turn granted him a percentage in gratitude. His extended stay in Egypt had given Hovsep a chance to observe and assess the country, and it made a lasting and favorable impression.

The massacres of 1894–1896, executed on the orders of Sultan Abdul Hamid II, known as "The Bloody Sultan", had left their mark on the Armenian population in Anatolia. Like many of his Armenian compatriots, Hovsep had witnessed those events and with the prospect of raising a young family, he felt unsafe. He decided to emigrate to Egypt with his new family. By then, he and Maritza had a daughter,

Varvar, born in 1892 and a son, Harootyoun, born in 1894. They would eventually have seven children in all. He wanted to take his family and go.

Hovsep's mother, who was living with them, was displeased and objected to her only son going away. So she accompanied them all the way to Samsun, from where they were supposed to take a ship bound for Egypt. Maritza, who had lost her own mother at a very young age, was close to her mother-in-law and her pleas had an effect. After spending about six months in Samsun, Maritza managed to convince Hovsep not to emigrate. As time went by, Hovsep became accustomed to Samsun and enjoyed its cultural diversity: a large European presence, consisting mainly of French and Greeks co-existed with the varied local population. So Hovsep soon opened his own shop in Samsun and began to thrive. Being an educated man, who used to entertain frequently, he had many Turkish friends and was well liked. He counted among his friends the District Governor of Samsun, Suleiman Nedjmi Bey.

It was in Samsun that Hovsep and Maritza had the rest of their children. Before Nonna was born, Maritza had given birth to a boy, named

Puzant, who had died at a very early age. A few years later, came a sister, Angèle, then a younger brother, Pierre, followed by Paul, who also died very young.

In early 1915, with Europe embroiled in the First World War, the first hint of the misfortune that would befall Nonna's family came to pass. Years later, when my mother, in her teens, stayed at her Grandmother Maritza's house, she listened with awe to these stories.

Hovsep was a guest at a well-attended government function in Samsun: a function in which he found he was the only non-Turk. In the course of the evening, he suddenly realized that talk had declined to whisper. Hovsep strained his ears unobtrusively and managed to grasp a few words here and there: one word that resonated particularly was the word *gavours*, a derogatory term meaning "unbelievers", "infidels" or "Christians". When his hosts, his friends, noticed his discomfort, they said "Hovsep, we're not talking about you." He replied "Of course, you're only saying that because I am here."

On returning home that night, he was agitated and paced up and down for hours. He did not sleep that night. He knew something was brewing and he knew it was not good news for the Armenians.

Not very long afterwards, perhaps a month later, three of his close Turkish friends, among them Suleiman Nedjmi Bey, came home to see him.

"Look, Hovsep, we've received instructions from Istanbul that all Armenians are to be deported," said Nedjmi Bey quietly and with a tone betraying grave concern. The District Governor had always liked Hovsep and felt compelled to help his friend. "If you become a Muslim, we promise to take you and your family from one mountain top to the other and we will defend you with our lives," he said.

"Can you hear the bombardment?" said one of the other friends. "The Russians are bombarding us from their warships. If they were to suddenly conquer us, to save my skin I would make the sign of the cross and convert to Christianity. At my age, do you really think I could become a real Christian believer? Obviously not, but if I have to save my skin, I will."

"I will not wear the veil!" said Maritza, with steely moist eyes and quivering lips.

"Then don't go out during the day, go out at night," replied Nedjmi Bey.

Hovsep was not convinced about it, so one of his friends painted a picture for him.

"You see all these children of yours? You are going to drop them on the way: one at a time."

Hovsep said he would think about their advice, discuss it with his whole family and let them know his decision.

Once his friends had left, Hovsep gathered his family to discuss the matter. His eldest son, Harootyun, who was now 21, declared that he would not pull a black curtain across his family, by which he meant that they would not live in darkness: in a non-Christian world. He was adamant that he would not change religion.

"I will kill you one by one and then I will kill myself, but we will not become Muslims," he declared.

When you have a family, you can ill afford the luxury of principles. Nevertheless, Hovsep reluctantly agreed, knowing that in the depths of his soul, he had made the right decision no matter what happened. Soon enough, deportation orders arrived and the orders stated that all Armenians were supposed to go to the Syrian frontier for safety: safety for the Turks, because they were led to believe that Armenians were seeking independence.

Those Armenians who could afford it could go in coaches and those who couldn't were compelled to walk up to the Syrian border, traversing the harsh landscape of Anatolia. So for a few days and nights, Hovsep's family, like all the Armenians in Anatolia, prepared themselves for their unspeakable fate. They sewed their gold coins inside pouches and belts, which they would wear round their waists.

Hovsep was fortunate. He ordered two coaches: one for their goods and the other for themselves. So on that harrowing morning when all the Armenian people of Samsun gathered in the marketplace, awaiting their marching orders, Hovsep's Turkish friends, riding on their horses, came to wish him goodbye. They were sad: sad that Hovsep had not taken their advice. So the deportations began.

They traveled by day and at night they settled down in *khans* or Anatolian inns. They may have stopped to get some sleep, but no one slept. They talked and talked and talked. They wept. They worried. They wondered.

The next morning they got into the coaches and started off again. They traveled for an uncertain time until the coaches stopped at what looked like a military kiosk. The men were ordered to come down from the coaches. So Hovsep and his son, Harootyun, came down and were led away. The minute all the men had been taken away, the Turkish drivers whipped the horses and bolted away, with women and children screaming and wailing. This was only the beginning of the nightmare.

The coaches charged beneath the green mountains, across narrow and deep valleys, over fast-running and snow-clustered streams, above high plateaus and on the plains of the province of Sivas. The few silent witnesses to what was unfolding were the mute trees of the region: the oak trees, cluster pines and junipers. The coach did not stop until they arrived at a *khan* at night.

As soon as Maritza and her children came down from the coach, they realized that the coach that was laden with their goods had disappeared. Maritza panicked, went to the local telegraph

The honorable Turk: Nonna's story 19

office and sent a telegram to their friend, the District Governor Nedjmi Bey, saying she had lost her husband and son and would like to return home. The answer never came.

The coach started up again and soon arrived in Tokat. Here, Maritza had a sister who was married to a Kassabian, an uncle of Nonna's future husband. All the men of the family had disappeared, only the women remained. They were still there because one of the elder Kassabian girls was a teacher. We are told her parents had given her a very good education to compensate for her poor looks and limp. The Turks had kept her for the time being so that she could teach their children. Ultimately, they also perished.

Nonna's family could not stay in Tokat. So they went on and on until they came to a village called Charkeshla. It was springtime: the winter snow had melted and the hot rainless summer had not yet arrived. Some other Armenian families had also managed to stay on in this village.

Through acquaintances, they had heard that some Turks were sheltering women and families who had money, even though it was against the law. So Maritza, with her brood – Varvar, the eldest, aged 23, a young widow with a baby that would die on this journey, Victoria, 15, Angèle, 12 and Pierre 10 – also arranged to stay with a Turkish family.

They had heard rumors that certain Armenian families staying with Turkish families had disappeared or weren't living there anymore. It gave them cause for concern; they were alert. So when one fine morning, a young man, a member of the Turkish family they were staying with, invites the whole family to a picnic the next day, they accept reluctantly.

Back in their room, Nonna is beside herself and her eyes are frozen in panic. "I just know that they want to take us to the fields to kill us for our money. They know we have money because we were paying them rent." Silent for a few minutes, Nonna then emerged with a plan. She would be unwell the next day so they would have an excuse not to go out. In the morning, her mother put towels soaked in hot water on her face, making her face ruddy and hot. Thus, Nonna was able to feign illness and the whole family excused themselves from going on the picnic.

The honorable Turk: Nonna's story 21

In the afternoons, Pierre, who was a tall and lanky 10-year-old, with hair parted in the middle, used to go and play outside, in the town square, with the local Turkish children. One afternoon, he overheard the older boys saying that the local mayor had an important visitor for lunch and the visitor was the new Governor (*Vali*) of Sivas province, a man named Suleiman Nedjmi Bey. Alarm bells rang in Pierre's head and instinctively he knew he had to see the Nedjmi Bey and ask him for help.

He had no time to consult his family. There were two soldiers posted outside the mayor's office. Pierre tried to dive through one soldier's legs and when they tried to stop him, he started shouting and screaming. The mayor and Nedjmi Bey emerged from their office to see what the commotion was.

On seeing Nedjmi Bey, Pierre said: "Don't you recognize me, sir? I am Tchorbajian's son."

"Where's your family?" he quizzed. "Who are you with and where are you staying?"

"We are here. My mother and my sisters want to go back to Samsun. We sent you a telegram but we never got a reply," said Pierre.

So Nedjmi Bey turned round and murmured to the village mayor to send one of the guards with the boy to find out where they were staying. "Go to your mother and say I will be coming to see her after lunch." As Pierre walked away with the guard to return home, Nedjmi Bey whispered a few words to the village mayor.

As soon as the guard dropped Pierre off at his home, Nonna and her sisters pounced on him, chastising him for betraying them. When they calmed down to listen to his story, they couldn't believe Pierre's initiative. They waited and waited and waited for the new Governor.

After a few hours, Nedjmi Bey arrived at their house with the guard. They exchanged stories of events. He related his recent promotion to Governorship of Sivas province and Maritza narrated the loss of her husband and eldest son. He explained that he did receive their telegram but was unable to respond because they had already moved outside his jurisdiction.

"I'm on my way to Sivas to find a house before my family joins me in two weeks' time," said the Governor. "I will tell the village mayor to arrange for an extra coach so when my family comes, you will join my wife's coach to Sivas."

Soon after that he left. Just as he had promised, two weeks later, his family arrived in the village of Charkeshla and the Tchorbajian family joined them for the trip to Sivas.

On arriving at Sivas, the Governor called at an Armenian girls' school, which had been run by American Protestant missionaries. Whilst the building was still there, there was not a single pupil left. The only one left there was the headmistress, a woman by the name of Miss Mary Louise Graffam. He asked Miss Graffam if she would open one of the flats – in a building adjoining the school, which had previously housed the school doctor – and allow the Tchorbajians to stay there indefinitely. Miss Graffam obliged.

The Governor checked that Maritza had enough money, and provided her with an adequate supply of ration cards to buy bread. And so, Nonna and her family settled in the school in Sivas until the end of the War, under the protection of Miss Graffam.

Born in Monson, Maine on May 1871 and educated at Oberlin College, Ohio, Mary Louise Graffam was a teacher of mathematics, who had arrived in Asia Minor in 1901, aged 20, to

Mary Louise Graffam[2]
1871–1921

Suleiman Nedjmi Bey[3]
1871–1943

become the principal of the Girls' School in Sivas. Over the years, she learnt to speak Armenian, Turkish, French and German and used it to benefit others. In 1914, she was sent to Erzeroum to help in a military hospital and with no professional training, she was appointed head nurse at a Red Crescent Hospital, which she managed shrewdly, and earned much respect among the Turks. In 1915, when the Armenian deportations began, she set forth with "her people", about 3,000 who were connected with the mission and bore witness to the robbery, hunger, thirst, disease, kidnapping and murder committed against the Armenians. In Malatia, the Turks told her she could go no further and kept her there "in the worst description of hell" for three weeks before allowing her to return to Sivas. Her relationship with the Turks was inconsistent: she was once in court for treason and yet in 1917, the Ottoman government awarded her the Order of the Red Crescent praising her "self-devotion in the cause of the sick and ill-fated ones". In a letter to Oberlin College, James L Barton, secretary of the American Board of Commissioners for Foreign Missions wrote, "When the story of saints and martyrs of this war is written, high on the list will stand the name of Mary Graffam of the class of 1894."[4] After the war, she would resume her work in Sivas operating a farm for 70 orphan boys and a home for 160 rescued Armenian girls until her death at Sivas hospital on August 17, 1921.[5]

After Armistice Day, as Armenians were allowed to return to their homes, Maritza decided to go back to Tokat, on her own, to check on her three houses. She left Varvar, the eldest girl, who was now 26, in charge. In Tokat, they had a big house with a courtyard and two separate houses, which they used to rent, before the deportations. There was the family of a Turkish military man living in their house, but they told her they were leaving soon. So Maritza stayed in one of her other houses, until her house was available. Soon after, Nonna, her sisters and Pierre joined her. They stayed in their house and rented the other two. Even though Armenians were allowed to return to their towns and claim what they had, if they decided to leave Anatolia, they could take nothing with them: they had to leave everything behind.

In 1921–22, a new danger surfaced for the remaining Armenians in Anatolia. His name was Topal Osman, meaning Osman with a limp. Topal Osman pursued Armenians from village to village, from town to town, from city to city, killing them indiscriminately. The word among the general population was that he was a guerrilla fighter and that the government was unable to control him. Given the historical circumstances, we now know that this effort was to ensure surviving Armenians did not return to their Anatolian homeland. No doubt, as a reward for his services, the new Turkish Republic installed Topal Osman as head of security for the founder of their new republic, Mustapha Kemal, also known as Atatürk, meaning "Father of the Turks".

Maritza realized that there was no future for her daughters there. She decided that it was better to leave Anatolia. She told her three daughters to go to Egypt, the land that their father had dreamed of going to as a young man. She gave them money and said she would send them money regularly, even after they reached Egypt. They had relatives in Egypt, who had gone there before the war, and one in particular, a native of Tokat, named Matossian, who had made his name in tobacco plantations and production.

To board a ship to Egypt, Nonna and her sisters had to go to Istanbul. Even though they had relatives in Istanbul, it was a dangerous journey to undertake for three girls on their own. Fortunately for them, at that time, the Red Cross was in the process of gathering Armenian orphans who were still alive and taking them by ship to Greece and France. So Nonna and her sisters explained their predicament to the director of this Red Cross group and offered to pay for their travel costs. The Red Cross director, who understood their concerns and fears, accepted their monies and allowed them to travel with them to Istanbul.

On arrival in Istanbul, they were not permitted to disembark. They were compelled to board the orphanage ship. Knowing this in advance, they had sent word to Varvar's late husband's brother, a Jesuit priest called Père Pascal, who was serving in Istanbul, to come and escort them off the ship. So Père Pascal rented a boat, rowed to the ship and brought them down to Istanbul, where they stayed for almost a year waiting for the arrival of their Egyptian visas. They finally sailed for Egypt in 1923.

In Egypt, Nonna and her sisters settled down and started a new life. There was already a long-standing Armenian community there, whose numbers had now swelled with the survivors of the deportations. Within two years, Nonna met a young man called Simon Kassabian, a native of her father's town of Tokat, who was passing through Cairo on his way to Khartoum. He had heard that the Tchorbajian girls from Tokat were in Cairo and so he paid them a visit at home.

Simon was immediately struck by Nonna and soon asked for her hand in marriage. He shared with her his pain and loss. During the War, he had been working in Sudan with his uncles, because his father wanted him out of Anatolia. At the end of the War, he had returned home to look for his parents, only to learn that they had all perished. For reasons which are unclear, he had then gone to Mersin, a town on the Mediterranean coast, which after the War was administered by the French and invested all he had in setting up a shop selling cloth. When the French came to an arrangement with Atatürk

The honorable Turk: Nonna's story

Standing left to right: Pierre Tchorbajian, Simon and Victoria Kassabian and Angèle. Sitting: Maritza Tchorbajian, with my mother in her lap (Cairo, Egypt 1928)

and handed Mersin over to him, he was compelled to leave Mersin and lost everything.

When Nonna was engaged, she asked her mother to come to the wedding in Cairo and to stay on with her. So Maritza, accompanied by her son Pierre, left everything in Anatolia, and made her way to Egypt.

Years later, Maritza confided to her granddaughter, Mary, my mother, that she had never forgiven herself for being the cause of her husband's and son's death. Her reluctance to leave Samsun and her siding with her mother-in-law had prevented them going to Egypt before all the deportations began.

Nonna and Simon Kassabian lived their happy and quiet lives in Sudan. They had two children: a daughter, Mary, my mother, who was born in July 1927 and a son, George, who was born in December 1928.

Khartoum, Sudan, December 1966. I would return from my daily holiday ritual of tennis and swimming at the American Club to see Nonna sitting in an armchair in the living room of our air-conditioned apartment. Invariably her glazed

The honorable Turk: Nonna's story 31

eyes would be locked on the cloudless blue sky outside the large window, with her hands clasped and thumbs rolling in a circular backward motion. To this day I wonder what images her memory was throwing on her mind's screen. I wonder if she ever knew that her survival had depended on the friendship of a mass murderer. I wonder if it would have made a difference to her.

After a wonderful lunch cooked by Ahmed, our family cook who had cooked for my father since1939, Nonna would continue with her stories in bits and pieces, customarily washed down with Turkish coffee and baklava. I am grateful for these bitter-sweet memories.

In spite of all the turmoil in her life, Nonna was a happy and balanced woman. Whatever ill feeling she may have had, she must have let it go. She had no resentment against the Turks in general. I had promised her that I would write her story. She died on 20 September 1978 in Nice, France. Twenty-five or so years later, I have decided to take time out and write her story with a purpose that I believe she would have been proud of.

"I hate what the Turks did to us, but I do not hate the Turks"

> *Victoria Tchorbajian Kassabian – "Nonna"*
> *Khartoum, December 1966*

Notes

1 http://www.kafkas.org.tr/izbirakan/suleymannecmi.html

2 Photograph of Mary Louise Graffam from *Silences: My Mother's Will to Survive* by Alice Tashjian, Chapter 4, http://mothermillennia.org/tashjian/silences.ch4.html

3 Photograph of Suleiman Nedjmi Bey from http://www.kastamonu.gov.tr/html/valiler1.html

4 James L Barton's letter to W F Bohn, Oberlin College, Oberlin, dated April 13, 1917

5 Mary Louise Graffam of Sivas, Turkey, *Sketches of a Service Heroic and Consecrated* by Ethel D Hubbard, reprinted by Woman's Board of Missions, 503 Congregational House, Boston, Mass, pages 1–22, from the original *Lone Sentinels in the Near East* by same author.

PART II ◆ *The Present*

Protecting the truth

One day a neighbor wanted to borrow Nasreddin Hodja's donkey. The Hodja didn't want to lend it and told him that he had lent his donkey to a friend.

Just then, the donkey started to bray. The neighbor said: "But Hodja I can hear the donkey! It's in your stable."

The Hodja stayed cool and answered with dignity: "Who are you going to believe, me or the donkey?"[1]

This particular story of Nasreddin Hodja helps to highlight the official Turkish position on the Armenian genocide. The Hodja represents Turkey, the neighbor represents Armenia and the donkey represents the compelling evidence of "genocide". The Hodja and the neighbor, like the Turks and the Armenians, are protecting the truth.

Turkey, like the Hodja, not only expects the Armenians and the World to believe that no genocide occurred, but also becomes indignant and insulted, in spite of the compelling evidence.

A brief overview of the Turkish and Armenian perspectives is essential. This is then followed by the conclusions from three distinguished sources: an Armenian, a Turkish and an American, which show conclusively why "genocide" is the term for what happened in Anatolia in 1915 and why it's not only the descendents of the Armenian victims that bear the pain but also the descendents of their Turkish persecutors.

Scholars, on both sides of the divide, have worked to buttress their positions with research, examinations and cross-referenced documents across the world so that they can protect their truth. For the Turks, it is to show that what befell the Armenians was not genocide, but a tragedy – for which Armenians still await for an apology from the Turks, almost 90 years after the event. For the Armenians, nothing short of genocide is acceptable.

On the Turkish side, the position is that Ottoman Turkey was in the middle of a war of survival. The relocation of Armenians was a security measure to protect the empire and the number of Armenians that died in this period was no more than 300,000. With academic support from US scholars like Bernard Lewis, Justin McCarthy and Heath Lowry, the truth was protected from exposure, until now.

On the Armenian side, the position is that Ottoman Turkey premeditated the liquidation of all Armenians from Anatolia, which it wanted purely for itself. The liquidation of 1,500,000 Armenians – more than half of the world's Armenian population at that time from their ancestral homeland – is genocide.

There is a huge gap between the positions of both sides. The truth is being protected on both sides with diligence, passion and vigilance. So what is the truth?

The Turkish perspective

From the Turkish perspective, the European powers had helped to diminish the frontiers of the Ottoman Empire in Europe over the previous decades and were looking for fresh opportunities to carve up the eastern part of their empire. In retrospect and in view of the intentions of the Sykes-Picot Agreement of 1916 between Great Britain and France, this is not wholly untrue. The Germans and the Russians also had their eyes firmly fixed on the Ottoman lands and assets.

At the center of the Young Turk Revolution of 1908 stood the Committee of Union and Progress (CUP) *(Ittihad ve Terakki Jemiyeti)* formed in 1889. Its members came to be known as *Ittihadists* or Unionists. The most ideologically committed party in the entire Young Turk movement, the CUP espoused a form of Turkish nationalism which was xenophobic and exclusionary in its thinking. Its policies threatened to undo the tattered fabric of a multi-ethnic and multi-religious society.

The CUP – headed by a triumvirate consisted of Talaat Pasha, Enver Pasha and Djemal Pasha – believed that a besieged Turkish nation needed Anatolia as its homeland. The problem was that Anatolia was populated by a large proportion of non-Turks. This was especially true in the six eastern provinces, also known as the "Armenian" provinces of Erzurum, Van, Bitlis, Kharpert (Elazig), Sivas and Diyarbekir[2] – see map on the next page. The Armenians represented almost 40 per cent of the

The present: Protecting the truth

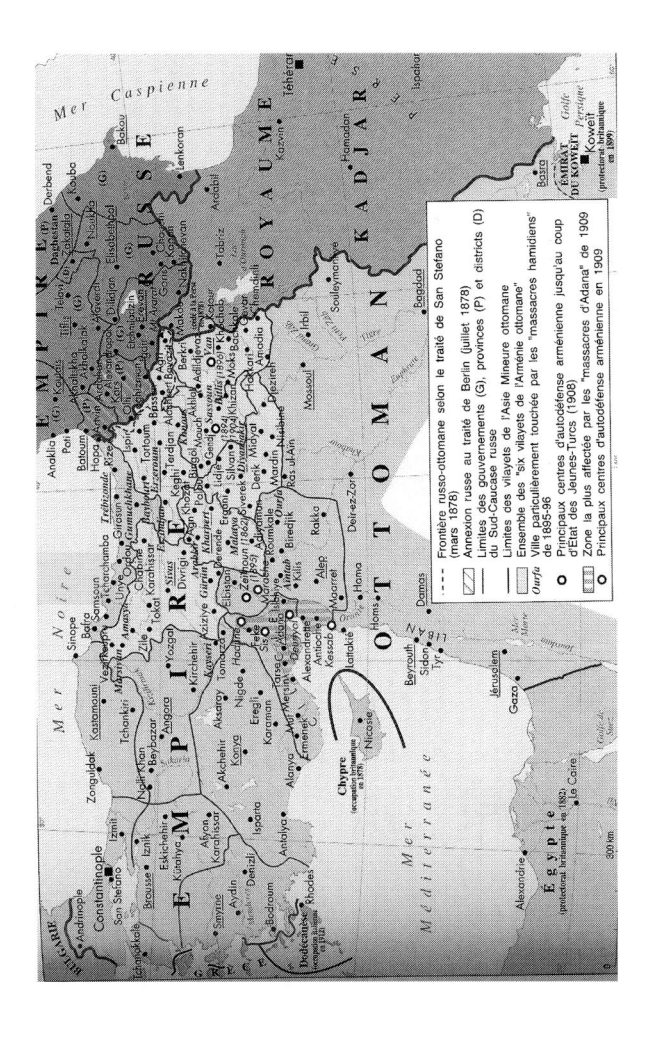

Map of the region on the eve of the First World War, 1914
The names of the six Armenian provinces are underlined: Van, Bitlis, Erzeroum, Diyarbekir, Kharpert, and Sivas.

Courtesy: "Atlas Historique de l'Armenie" by Claude Mutafian and Eric Van Lauwe
Published by Editions Autrement Paris 2001

population, while the Turks represented 25 per cent and the Kurds 15 per cent.[3] In the provinces hugging the Aegean Sea and Black Sea, the Greeks had a strong representation. The Armenian and Greek communities were, in their view, essentially a bone stuck in the throat of a new Turkey.

Turkey claims it was compelled to deport the Armenians to the Syrian border, because there were strong indications that Armenians in Turkey were collaborating with the Russians. Turkey had little choice but to protect itself and its people from present danger. They compare it to the internment of the Japanese-Americans during the Second World War.

At the end of the First World War, Ottoman Turkey was a defeated nation, and fearing retribution from the Allies, Atatürk and his friend and partner, Ismet Inönü, embarked on a campaign to take power in Turkey and snatch victory out of the jaws of defeat. With European powers focused on demobilizing their armies and lacking the appetite for battle with the Turks, Atatürk succeeded in taking power, with help from the rank-and-file criminals who, during the war, committed atrocities against the Armenians. In return, the nascent Turkish

Republic was compelled to protect these criminals and so it continued to finalize the liquidations started by the CUP.

"A unified and homogenous country, an atmosphere devoid of local and foreign constraints," stated Inönü, President of Turkey. "The name of this country is Turkey. This Turkey is defined by this treaty [of Lausanne]."[4] Atatürk and Inönü created a new Turkey out of the rubble of the Ottoman Empire. This was a new Turkey for Turks only. The Ottoman Empire was history and legally the new Turkey had severed connections to its past.

The Armenian perspective

From the Armenian perspective, Anatolia was their homeland for nearly 3,000 years, long before any Seljuk or Ottoman invasions. Over its entire existence, Armenia had little acquaintance with peace, but under the Ottomans they had a respite until the late 19th century; so much so that the Muslim Ottomans gave the Christian Armenians the accolade "the loyal nation" *(millet-i sadika)*.

On April 24, 1915, having muzzled their own

Parliament, Talaat Pasha, the mastermind of the Armenian genocide, ordered the arrest and liquidation of Armenian community leaders, intellectuals and writers in Istanbul. With the Armenian leaders destroyed, Talaat and his henchmen proceeded unhindered with orders for the deportation of the Armenian population at large in Anatolia. To minimize Turkish casualty, the men were separated from their families, and to save much-needed ammunition for the war effort, they were brutally butchered. Thereafter, Kurdish brigands and released convicts were set loose on defenseless women and children, who were kidnapped or raped, savaged and mutilated. One and a half million Armenians perished in this process. Those that survived the ordeal that summer, across the scorching desert into Syria, faced the prospect of a new life with trauma and denial.

Turkey had achieved its objective: an Anatolia virtually cleansed of Armenians. It would take the Armenians another 50 years to regain their strength and start a movement for recognition of these events as genocide. In general, if there were any Armenian acts of aggression, they would have been in self defense and in resistance to deportation and drowning, murder and mayhem, rape and robbery.

The present: Protecting the truth 41

VIA DOLOROSA

—(KIRBY) *New York World*, Dec., 1922

Courtesy: http://chgs.hispeed.com/Histories__Narratives__Documen/Armenian_Genocide/armenian_genocide.html

The Armenian population in Anatolia was a subject race in the Ottoman Empire and they were not permitted to carry weapons. The fact that they were not Muslims made them second-class citizens, with lesser rights. Civil war requires both sides to have the capacity to wage a war: Armenians were in no position to wage a civil war. Although the idea of an independent Armenia was an attractive proposition, for most Armenians living under the Turkish yoke, it was a most difficult dream. Armenian and European scholars assert that in the face of militant Islamic Turks, Christian Armenians were not only passive and weak, they were no match. Nevertheless, even acknowledging that there were Armenian *fedayees* or freedom fighters (martyrs for their homeland), and even if we were to assume that some or even a large proportion of the Armenian population was seeking independence, how can anyone justify genocide? Even good decent Turks recoiled at the events unfolding in front of them.

1 An Armenian academic proves genocide beyond any reasonable doubt

Compelling evidence that proves conclusively that the Ottoman government did in fact intend to exterminate the Armenians in Anatolia has been unearthed by Professor Vahakn Dadrian, an Armenian-American scholar, who has spent a lifetime researching this subject in the US, in Europe and in Turkey and Armenia. He has also written a number of books on the subject, including *The History of the Armenian Genocide* (1995) and *The Key Elements in the Turkish Denial of the Armenian Genocide: A Case Study of Distortion and Falsification* (1999).

Dadrian's methodology to prove his case is that "It has to be documentation of a special kind that overwhelms the deniers." He himself states that compelling evidence must be reliable, explicit, incontestable and verifiable. To avoid all accusations of victim-bias, Dadrian avoids using the massive volume of individual and authentic Armenian survivor sources. Nor does he use British, French and Russian archives, which are also full of authentic documents, but because these powers were enemies of Ottoman Turkey in the First World War, it could invite accusations of war propaganda. Neither does he use any of the materials written and collected by the Protestant, Catholic and other Christian sources, so as not to invite accusations of religious bias.

So where did Dadrian find compelling evidence that proves beyond any doubt that the Ottoman government in 1915 had in fact premeditated, organized and executed, with extreme brutality, the liquidation of the Armenian people from Anatolia?

Compelling evidence from German and Austrian archives

In a speech delivered at Harvard University on 24 April 2001, Dadrian produced two classes of documentation, which met his restricted criteria. The first is documents extracted from the Imperial archives of the allies of the Ottoman Empire during the First World War: Imperial Germany and Imperial Austria-Hungary. In 18 visits over 20 years, Dadrian compiled many hundreds of German and Austro-Hungarian documents, detailing graphically the daily atrocities taking place in the interior of Turkey at the time. These documents were produced by German and Austro-Hungarian officials: consuls, vice-consuls and military officers. The strategic and compelling significance of these German and Austrian documents is that they were not intended for public consumption. These were wartime reports meant to be used by the superiors of these officers for internal use.

"It is inconceivable that a military and political ally, during war, would venture to discredit another ally. On the contrary, German and Austrian officials went out of their way to protect the reputation of Turkey," says Dadrian.

"When you read these documents again and again, the single word used by ambassador after ambassador – Wagenheim, Hohenlohe, Metternich and Bernstorffe – is the German word *'Ausrottung'*, which means purely and simply 'extermination'."[5]

Compelling evidence from Ottoman archives

The second class of compelling evidence is provided by two distinct authentic Turkish documents. The first emanates from the 1919–21 court martials held in Istanbul and the Mazhar Inquiry Commission, which was invested with extraordinary powers of subpoena and arrest. These were stamped "It conforms to the original" in Turkish at the top of the documents. Dadrian further reconfirms the authenticity of these Turkish documents because even here, the Ottoman prosecutors disregarded Armenian survivor testimony in these courts and inquiries. Here is one example of military communications that are difficult to misinterpret.

The Military commander at Bogazlžyan, a district in Ankara province, sends a cipher telegram to his superior in Ankara, Colonel Recayi. He says: "Today we dispatched so many Armenians to their destination."

Colonel Recayi, pretending not to understand, wires back saying: "What do you mean, 'dispatched to their destination'?" The answer comes within an hour: "They were killed off."

The second category of Turkish official documents involves parliamentary debates. For about seven weeks in October, November and December 1918, the senate and lower house debated the Armenian deportations and massacres. Several deputies came to confess the crimes of massacres against the Armenians. The President of the Ottoman Senate, Ahmed Riza, a former Young Turk himself, made this declaration: "We Turks savagely killed off the Armenians."

On November 21, 1918, in the same senate, the most remarkable revelation was made by another senator, Resid Akif, an Ottoman statesman. "I was a member of the first post-war Ottoman government. One day in my office, I came across two types of documents. One was the official order of the Interior Ministry, Talaat, ordering the deportation of the Armenians, in which Talaat is telling his subordinates, 'protect the Armenian deportee convoys – give them olives and bread'."

The present: Protecting the truth 47

But parallel to this, an informal order goes out, not issued by any government agency, but what sociologists call "informal authority", namely the central Committee of the CUP. Resid Akif continues, "The order was simple. As soon as the Armenian convoys leave their villages and towns and cities, proceed with the execution of the mission." Akif Pasha says the mission was for these criminals to attack the convoys and massacre the population.[6]

What determines genocide?

Dadrian points out four determinants of genocide: first, premeditation, second, intent, third, organization and fourth, execution.

First, the most devastating evidence of premeditation comes from the Turkish martial proceedings produced in the legal journal of the Ottoman Parliament, *Takvim-I Vekyi*, number 3540, page 8:

"There is evidence that one of the architects of the Armenian genocide, Doctor Nazžm, had warned Governor Jelal of Aleppo to the effect that the anti-Armenian measures were not the result of impulsive decision-making but the product of 'profound and long deliberations' *(ariz ve amik dusunlerek)."* Jelal responded: "I can deport the Armenians, but I cannot have them massacred! I cannot soil my hands with the blood of innocent people." He was soon relieved of his post.

Second, genocidal intent is explicit in Turkish, German and Austro-Hungarian documents, mentioned earlier.

Third, the organization of the genocide was unprecedented in the annals of legal justice. It was not government officials as such, but "informal authority", CUP party functionaries, who dominated the government and acted as unofficial adjuncts to the government.

Lastly, the execution of the Armenian genocide was the "final solution". The two major perpetrators and architects of the genocide – Dr Nazžm and Dr Sakir – repeatedly declared: "Sultan Abdel Hamid did an unfinished job; we cannot be satisfied with partial results, therefore in order to be complete, drastic and definitive about the destruction of the Armenians, we need criminals. We have to be merciless with the women and children."

In February 1916, the Turkish High Command

The present: Protecting the truth 49

appointed General Vehip commander of the Third Army with jurisdiction over the six major Armenian provinces. Vehip had sent a 2,500-man Armenian labor battalion from Sivas to Adana to help with the Baghdad Railway. When he discovered that not only had they not reached their destination, but that they had been brutally massacred, he established a court martial and hanged the two perpetrators of the massacre.

In his affidavit, General Vehip gives detailed description of how Dr Sakir went from province to province in a private car giving orders. He describes the release from the prisons of the most brutal, fiendish criminals *(ipten ve kazžkdan kurtulmus yaranžnz)*.

He then describes a scene of atrocity that epitomizes the quintessence of the Armenian genocide. When he went to Mus, in Bitlis province, he visited Tchurig, an Armenian village, five kilometers north of Mus. He describes what he saw: "In all the wooden houses of that village, Armenian women and children were crowded and burned alive. I saw their charred remains." He concludes with: "In the history of Islam, you cannot find any parallel to such fiendishness and savagery." These are the words of a respected Ottoman Army Commander.[7]

Who defines genocide?

Let's take a look at three perspectives: the originator of the word "genocide", the United Nations and the declarations of Holocaust and genocide scholars.

First, the man who coined the term "genocide" in 1944 was Raphael Lemkin, who was the earliest proponent of the Genocide Convention invoking the Armenian case as a definitive example of genocide in the 20th century. He described the crime as a systematic destruction of whole, national, racial, or religious groups. The sort of thing Hitler did to the Jews and the Turks to the Armenians.[8]

Second, when the United Nations (UN) adopted the first resolution on genocide, on Lemkin's urging, on 11 December 1946, the UN General Assembly resolution (96-1) and the UN Genocide Convention itself recognized the Armenian genocide itself as a type of crime the UN intended to prevent by codifying existing standards.[9]

The present: Protecting the truth

Third, at a meeting of the Association of Genocide Scholars in 1997, the Association as a whole officially voted a resolution that the Armenians had been subject to full-scale genocide. Moreover, in 2000, at a Conference on the Holocaust held in Philadelphia, a large number of researchers on the Holocaust, including Israeli historians, signed a public declaration that the Armenian genocide was factual. So when Shimon Peres, Israeli Foreign Minister, in an effort to shore up Turkish-Israeli friendship, declared in April 2001 that what happened to the Armenians was a tragedy but not a genocide, Israel Charny, the world's pre-eminent genocide scholar and an Israeli citizen, rebuked him for stooping so low.[10]

Why would all these people cast aspersions against the Turks? Is it because they hate Turkey and want to harm it? Are they liars and cheats? Do they have nothing better to do? Perhaps the questions one should ask are: Why is Turkey failing in silencing its enemies, who accuse it of such horrific crimes? Why is Turkey afraid to go to an International Court or Tribunal? Why were the Turks not told about this? Why is this information hidden from them? Who is being protected? How can we find the whole truth and resolve this issue? Do we really want to know the truth? If the average Turk had the courage to face the Truth, if they really wanted to know the truth, they would come to the same conclusions as Dr Taner Akcam, a courageous and honorable Turk.

2 A Turkish historian discovers that the Republic of Turkey is implicated

"Perhaps that is because so many of the murderers and looters were also heroes of the founding of the modern Turkish republic," declares Dr Taner Akcam, a Turkish historian and sociologist and author of *Dialogue across an International Divide: Essays towards a Turkish-Armenian Dialogue*.

Akcam reckons that one of the main obstacles to a public debate in Turkey is collective amnesia. Atatürk severed the lines connecting the Turkish people to their past. Through a series of reforms, such as westernization of dress codes and with the adoption of the Latin alphabet in 1928, they tried to erase the traces of the recent past. Events prior to 1928 and the writings, in Arabic script, of the past generations became a closed book.

The present: Protecting the truth 53

Turkish history between 1878 and 1918 was an era of dishonor and humiliation, when Ottoman rulers lost 85 per cent of their lands and 75 per cent of their population. The Ottoman elite saw the First World War as a historic opportunity to regain its former grandeur and recover its national pride. That illusion fast vanished. The Armenians became substitute enemies for the Great Powers. "Ottoman leaders did not just purge this period of trauma by rewriting history and refashioning a new national identity. They also managed to blot out its memory and stifle any initiative that could impinge on this organized amnesia," writes Akcam. "The Turks have not been able to construct an identity purged of the old trauma."

There are several links between the founding of the Republic and the Armenian massacres and these have also done much to make the subject taboo. Leading figures connected to the republic have spoken publicly on the issue.

A well known member of the CUP party, Halil Mentese, said: "If we had not cleansed eastern Anatolia of the Armenian militia, who collaborated with the Russians, the founding of our national republic would not have been possible." At the Republic's first National

Assembly, speeches were made on the themes of "We took the risk of being thought of as murderers to save the fatherland."

"As you know, the question of deportation was an event that provoked the reaction of the whole world and made us all seem like murderers," said Hasan Fehmi, a Deputy and later Finance Minister in the new Ankara cabinet. "We knew before we launched this action, that we would be subjected to the anger and hatred of the Christian world. Why did we allow our name to be mixed up with the opprobrium of a reputation of murderers? Why did we take on such a huge and difficult task? Because we had to do what was necessary to preserve the fatherland and future of our country, which in our eyes are more precious and sacred than our lives."

With time, official history was changed to one of anti-imperialism and respect for the resistance troops during the war of national independence. A debate on the genocide would end up by showing that the state was not a product of an anti-imperialist struggle, but a war conducted against the Armenian and Greek minorities. The genocide of the Armenians was inextricably linked with the resistance in Anatolia: the members who perpetrated the genocide were able to transform themselves into resistance troops *(kuvay-i-milliye)*.

The second link between the emergent republic and the genocide came from a class enriched as a result of the genocide, which came to constitute one of the social bases of the nationalist movement. The leading families or "notables", who had prospered from the looting, feared that the Armenians would return to take back their possessions and take revenge. That is what happened in the Cukurova region, where the surviving Armenians returned with the occupation forces to take back what belonged to them. So the notables merged with the national liberation movement and even organized it in some places. Some of them were even close to Atatürk: for example, Topal Osman – you may recall him from Nonna's story – became commander of his personal guard. Measures passed by the old Constantinople (Istanbul) government on 8 January 1920 for the restitution of Armenian possessions was cancelled on 14 September 1922. The new government in Ankara, which became Turkey's capital in October 1923, realized the need to look after the interests of those who had contributed to the founding of the state.

There is also a third link between the genocide and the republic: some of the organizers and top officials of the first resistance troops were wanted for taking part in the massacres. In organizing the resistance, Atatürk had been actively assisted by members of the CUP party, wanted for crimes against the Armenians.

Sukru Kaya, minister of the interior and secretary general of the People's Republican Party *(Cumhuriyet Halk Partisi)*, founded by Atatürk, was in charge of settling immigrant and nomadic populations at the time of the "deportations". His position made him officially responsible for organizing the deportation. The German consuls present recorded Sukru Kaya's words: "We must exterminate the Armenian race."

Mustafa Abdulhalik Renda was governor of Bitlis, then of Aleppo, during the massacres. The German consul Rössler describes him as someone "relentlessly taken up with the destruction of the Armenians." He later became a minister and president of the National Assembly.

Arif Fevzi, detained in Malta (prisoner number 2743) for having organized the Diyarbekir massacres, became a minister from 1922 to

1923. Ali Cenani Bey (prisoner number 2805) who profited materially from the genocide was minister of trade from 1924 to 1926. Rüshtü Aras, a member of the sanitary commission in charge of burying Armenians who had been killed, later held high positions in Ankara: he was foreign minister from 1925 to 1938.

For the "wanted" party members, in particular those from the Special Organization – consisting of released criminals – which actually committed the massacres, joining the war of independence was a matter of survival. Just imagine the Second World War did not end the way we know it. Let's say Germany had not totally collapsed because let's say Field-Marshall Rommel, with the help of the SS and Nazi troops, had repulsed the Allies in 1943 and then signed a peace treaty with the Allies to end the war, leaving Germany intact. Naturally, Rommel would have been compelled to pardon the Nazis for their valuable contribution to the fatherland. Now can you imagine the Jews trying to convince the Germans to accept that the Third Reich had committed a holocaust against them?

Admitting today that there were murderers and thieves among those heroes who saved Turkey would certainly have a shattering effect. Denial is an easier path for those who fear shaking the Turks' belief in the republic and its national identity. For Turkey to face the future without fear, it must confront the ghosts of its past. Without doing so, Turkey and its people are condemned to remain in a quagmire.[11]

"If you can't bring yourself to describe it as genocide, call it a massacre. But it was a crime against humanity… Ask forgiveness from the Armenian people," said Akcam on a remarkable debate televised nationwide in Turkey in March 2001. On the same day, in the leading Turkish newspaper *Milliyet*, Yavuz Baydar wrote that "these men [the Young Turk leaders] are our Pol Pots, Berias and Stalins, and the sooner we call these crimes to account, the better our chances of redeeming ourselves from this scourge of being accused of genocide."[12]

3 An American journalist dreams in Turkish

"Something about the concept of diversity frightens Turkey's ruling elite," writes Stephen Kinzer, who was for many years Istanbul bureau chief for The New York Times, a Turcophile and author of *Crescent and Star: Turkey between Two*

The present: Protecting the truth 59

Worlds. "It triggers the deep insecurity that has gripped Turkish rulers ever since the republic was founded in 1923, an insecurity that today prevents Turkey from taking its proper place in the modern world." [13]

Its current leaders do not believe that Turks can be trusted with the fate of their nation. They believe that their people are not mature enough. Turkey has become an entirely different nation. Villages have become cities, cow paths have become super highways. Universities and public hospitals are to be found even in the most remote regions. The economy is unsteady but productive, with corporations making vast amounts of money and competing globally. The people are educated, self-confident and eager to build a nation that embodies the ideals of democracy and human rights.

"The ruling elite, however, refuses to embrace this new nation or even admit it exists. Military commanders, prosecutors, security officers, narrow-minded bureaucrats, lapdog newspaper editors, rigid conservative politicians and other members of this sclerotic cadre remain psychologically trapped in the 1920s," says Kinzer. They see threats from across every one of Turkey's eight borders and, most dangerously, from within the country itself. In their minds, Turkey is still a nation under siege. To protect it from mortal danger, they feel obliged to run it themselves. They not only ignore but actively resist intensifying pressure from educated worldly Turks who want their country to break free of its shackles and complete its march toward democracy that was Atatürk's dream.[14]

Until this dilemma is resolved, Turkey will live in eternal limbo: in half a democracy. "In 1980, before returning to their barracks, the military wrote a new constitution, which effectively bolstered them and has been used to prevent the flowering of Turkish democracy," writes Kinzer. "This rationale for limiting democracy is repeated constantly in Turkey. After a while it begins to sound like what an overprotective mother might say about her child. No mother would allow her four-year-old to cross the street alone or handle knives or play with matches, but there comes a time when, however reluctantly, she accepts that her child has grown up and is able to handle the responsibilities of adulthood. The fear of popular will that underpins Turkey's political system is like that of a mother whose child turns fifteen and then eighteen and then twenty-five and older, but is still not trusted to leave home alone." [15]

The present: Protecting the truth 61

"Writers, journalists and politicians who criticize the status quo are packed off to prison for what they say or write," writes Kinzer. Calls for religious freedom are considered subversive attacks on the secular order. Expressions of ethnic or cultural identity are banned for fear that they will trigger separatist movements and ultimately rip the country apart. With 80 per cent of the total circulation of Turkish newspapers and many of the country's most powerful broadcast outlets controlled by two industrial groups that function very much like a cartel, there is little room for maneuver.[16]

If Turkey is to be transformed, it will require more than political reform. It will require Turks to change the way they view themselves and their relationship to society. In Turkey the individual is considered less important than the family or village or clan. Their leaders long ago bound them together by creating a concept called *devlet*. "This is my least favorite Turkish word," says Kinzer. "The dictionary says it means 'state', but it also means something much uglier. *Devlet* is an omnipotent entity that stands above every citizen. Loyalty to it is a most fundamental obligation and questioning it is treasonous. Its guardians are the self-perpetuating elite: the generals, the police chiefs, prosecutors, judges, political bosses and press barons. Freethinkers threaten *devlet*. It is Turkey's apocalyptic swordsman, the repressive mentality that overwhelms, constricts and suffocates the citizenry." [17]

In today's Turkey, no two words are as fundamentally contradictory as *istiklal* (freedom) and *devlet* (state or nation) says Kinzer. The first stands for freedom and progress and the second is the dark force that represents fear, mistrust and arrogance. It keeps Turkey in chains. For Turkey to live, *devlet* must die.

One central factor that contributes to the tension between *istiklal* and *devlet*, which Kinzer does not focus on, is the Armenian genocide. The freedom that Turkey obtained in the 1920s was stained with innocent blood of the Armenians. It was tainted freedom; a freedom stolen, not earned. Atatürk's Republic was organized with the invaluable support of mass murderers and thieves, who needed concealment and protection for their crimes and ill-gotten gains. The concept of *devlet* is not unlike the family rules of the Italian-American mafia, where there was honor among thieves and "breaking the silence" meant swift retribution. To this day, *devlet* protects the descendants of these criminals and the Turkish nation will remain captive until they can shake these chains off. Nobody can help them: only they can help themselves because this is an internal struggle.

From a mental or spiritual aspect, Turkey could be compared to a prison, where Turks are incarcerated with their prison guards – the military establishment – who live quite happily in the prison. The prison doors are locked from the inside and the keys are held by the wardens. Is it not strange that these prisoners generally disagree on just about every conceivable issue they face, except the Armenian genocide?

"Turkey may have the strongest army in the Middle East, but it has been proven powerless against a fictive attack far costlier than bombing. And 20 years later, the bombs are still falling!" wrote Haluk Sahin, one of Turkey's top TV journalists.[18] This fictive attack he writes about is nothing less than the film *Midnight Express*, which seared in the mind's eye of a whole generation in the West the picture of Turks as brutal creatures. One can actually empathize with the frustration the Turks feel at what they see as gross injustice to their sense of integrity. What Mr Sahin perhaps does not realize is that he is experiencing a fraction of the frustration Armenians have lived with when their pain and loss has been denied for nearly a hundred years. Today, the Turkish authorities are powerless once more against the film *Ararat*, directed by Canadian-Armenian film producer Atom Egoyan, which depicts the events of 1915. In truth, the film will help the Turkish people reach a new awareness, see a new interpretation and perhaps even shift to a new understanding.

"For Turkey to live, *devlet* must die," wrote Kinzer. The key to killing *devlet* is for Turkey to acknowledge the guilt on the Armenian genocide and to seek reconciliation. In so doing, it will set us – Armenians and Turks – free from protecting the truth.

"Divine justice may be delayed, but it cannot be forfeited (Adaleti Allahiyede imhal var ihmal yoktur)"

General Vehip Pasha
Commander-in-Chief, Ottoman Third Army, 1918

The present: Protecting the truth 65

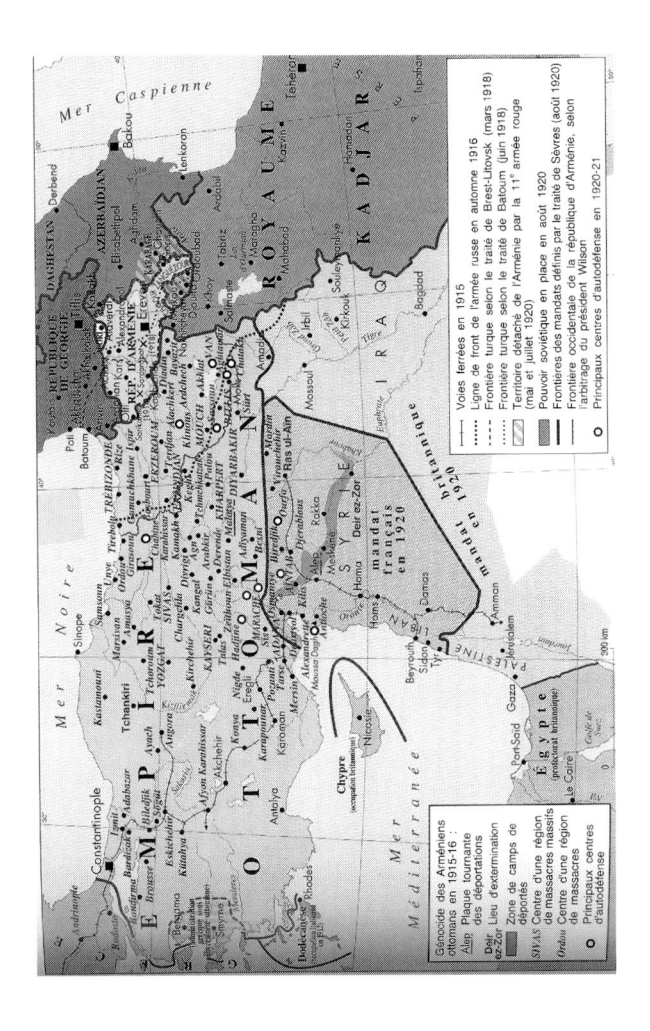

Map of the region following the Treaty of Sèvres 1920.
The black dots represent towns ethnically cleansed, and towns in capital letters represent centers of large-scale massacres.

Courtesy: "Atlas Historique de l'Armenie" by Claude Mutafian and Eric van Lauwe
Published by Editions Autrement Paris 2001

Notes

1 http://www.turkishodyssey.com/turkey/culture/heroes.htm
   Nasreddin Hodja was a 13th century Anatolian master of folk humor, whose anecdotes used incisive humor, insightful satire and self-criticism to make people more aware and help them cope.

2 The current Turkish provinces of Erzurum, Van, Bitlis, Elazig, Sivas and Diarbekir are configured differently.

3 Statistical analysis of the racial elements in the Ottoman Vilayets of Erzerum, Van, Bitlis, Mamouret-el-Aziz, Diyarbekir and Sivas. Drawn up in 1912 by the Armenian Patriarchate at Constantinople.

4 http://www.mfa.gov.tr/grupk/words.htm,
   75th Anniversary of the Turkish Republic, Republic of Turkey, Ministry of Foreign Affairs.

5 Professor Vahakn Dadrian's lecture at Harvard University on April 24, 2001:
   http://groong.usc.edu/news/msg47788.html

6 Ibid

7 Ibid

8 Responses to the letter from the Turkish Ambassador to the US, *The Key Elements in the Turkish Denial of the Armenian Genocide: A Case Study of Distortion and Falsification*, by Vahakn N Dadrian, published by the Zoryan Institute, Canada 1999, page 71

9 Ibid, page 72

10 Letter to Hon Shimon Peres, Foreign Minister, State of Israel, from Professor Israel W Charny, Executive Director, Institute on the Holocaust and Genocide, Jerusalem, Israel, Editor-in-Chief, *Encyclopedia of Genocide*.

11 *The long-denied Armenian Genocide: Turkey's carefully forgotten History* by Dr Taner Akcam, *Le Monde Diplomatique*, September 2001

12 *Of Genocides, Massacres, and Tragedies*, Gwynne Dyer, *Jordan Times*, Media Monitors Network, August 30, 2001

13 *Dreaming in Turkish*, Stephen Kinzer, *World Policy Journal*, v. 18 No 3 (Fall 2001) page 1

14 Ibid., page 3

15 Ibid., page 6

16 Ibid., page 8

17 Ibid., page 11

18 *"Midnight Express" 20 Years Later: A Turkish Nightmare*, by Haluk Sahin, *New Perspectives Quarterly*, Fall 1998, Volume 15, No 5, pages 21–22

PART III ◆ *The Future*

I have a dream

Scenario plans are specially constructed stories about the future. Each scenario represents a distinct plausible world. The purpose of scenario planning is not to predict the future but to prepare for the future. The use of scenario planning lies in its ability to challenge conventional wisdom and anticipate the future. The future belongs to those who prepare for it. This is my scenario plan or as I call it, "I have a dream".

Ankara, Turkia, 2023. Turkia is the new official name for Turkey and it has a new constitution, where individual liberty is recognized and encouraged. Even its flag was altered, so that the old flag was placed in the top left hand corner and the remaining area was covered with red and white horizontal stripes. Turkia is still not a member of the European Union, even though the Euro is Turkia's second currency. In the provinces, where there is a large Kurdish presence, the Kurdish language flourishes

The future: I have a dream 69

alongside the Turkish, not only in homes, but in public buildings, public communications and public networks. For the first time in Turkia's history, individuals have confidence in the economy, because they trust their government. This was not always so.

Turkia's population today is nearly 100 million. Twenty years ago it was nearly 70 million. With a teeming population, aggravated by 1,500,000 new births each year – ironically the same number that perished in the Armenian genocide – something had to give. The demographic problem combined with Turkey's constant and consistent economic downturns created a lethal cocktail that exploded in 2012. Russia with its oilfields was now an entrenched ally of the United States and Turkey became less and less of a strategic partner for the West. This was further aggravated by the support given to the US military by Uzbekistan and Tajikistan in the war on Afghanistan's Taliban regime back in 2002.

What followed was not dissimilar to the fall of the Ceauşescu regime in Romania. In the ensuing saga, the old generals were shown the door by the new generals. These new generals, educated in business, law and communications in universities in the EU and in the US, understood that Turkey had to finally say goodbye to Atatürk's legacy and move on into the real world of democracy, individual liberty and economic prosperity.

Like Spain's Franco and Russia's Lenin, Atatürk was consigned to history. Even though Atatürk himself was reputed to have been against the idea of being venerated after death, his followers and particularly the armed forces proceeded to enshrine Atatürk as the "eternal sultan" to ensure security, stability and suppression of the Turkish people.

One of the new generals, General X, who had studied law and journalism in the US, also understood that this "dawn" could not come about without some hard decisions: decisions that impacted on the past and the future. He resigned from the military on amicable terms and with their tacit approval, he formed a new civilian party. He invited and encouraged the leading economists, lawyers and writers to join him. He won a resounding victory at the general elections of 2013, on the platform of a new constitution that would transport Turkia into the 21st century. He ensured that the military was, constitutionally, legally and in reality, the servant and not the master of the Republic.

In time, President X and his civilian government made some far-reaching decisions that would shatter the old inflexible paternalistic culture – that was stifling not just the economy but the people's desire for more freedom of expression – and replace it with a more tolerant and flexible culture. Two issues hampered the execution of this. One was the Armenians abroad and the other was the Kurds at home. The public relations advisers of President X soon came up with a cunning plan not only to amicably resolve the Armenian and Kurdish issues, but to use them as catalysts to propel Turkey's future growth.

So it was arranged and in early 2015, Turkey recognised the Armenian genocide. On April 24 of that same year, the new Turkish President X flew to Yerevan to attend the special 100th anniversary ceremony at the Armenian Genocide memorial. The world stood still, stunned at these new developments. The impossible had happened. After 100 years of denial, Turkia had finally come round and recognized the Armenian genocide for what it was. Real change, real growth was about to happen, with political, social and economic catalysts at work. Let's take a look at the political catalysts.

Political catalysts

Turkish admission of genocide opened the much-feared debate on land and reparations. Much debate raged on everywhere. These ranged from extremist Turks not wanting to cede any lands to extremist Armenians wanted all six provinces returned. Official referendums in the Armenian Diaspora and in Armenia and Turkia delivered a majority vote for a final, realistic and mutually-acceptable settlement. Representatives of the Republics of Turkia and Armenia, the Armenian Diaspora and Nagorno-Karabakh thrashed out a final settlement.

Turkia ceded back to Armenia a slither of territory that the Soviet Union had handed over to Kemalist Turkey under terms agreed in the Treaty of Moscow and Kars in 1921. These territories included Kars, Ardahan, Ani, Artvin and some shoreline on the Black Sea, giving Armenia access to the Black Sea.

Turkia, through its Genocide Reparations Council, also agreed to pay sensible reparations

The future: I have a dream 73

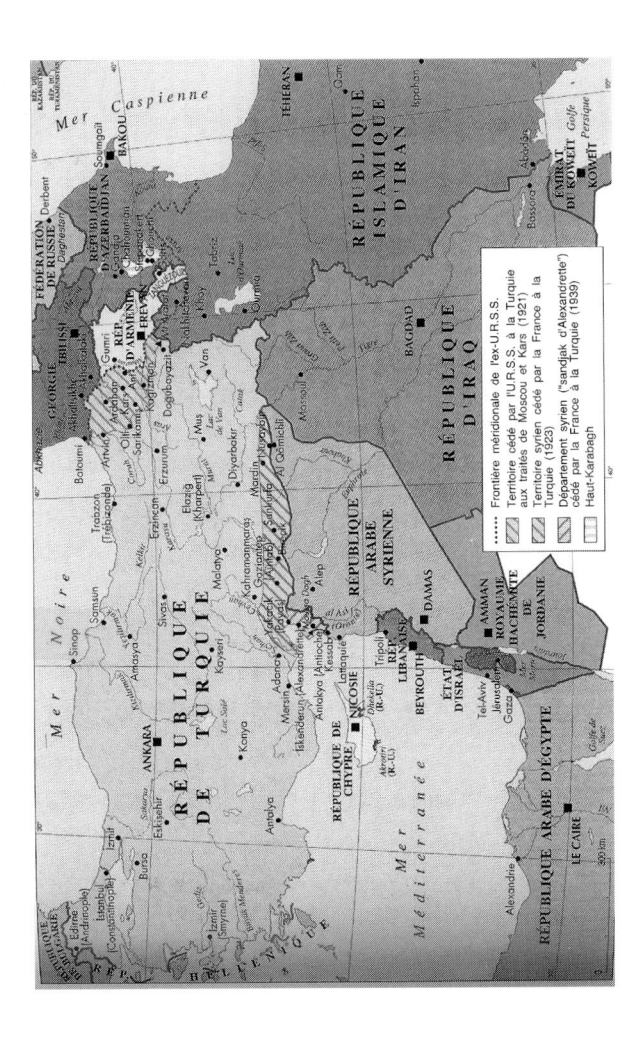

Map of the region at the dawn of the 21st century
The Soviets ceded Armenian lands including Ani, Kars, and
Ardahan to Turkey in 1921 – shown above in stripes

Courtesy: "Atlas Historique de l'Armenie" by Claude Mutafian and Eric Van Lauwe
Published by Editions Autrement Paris 2001

to the Armenian Diaspora of an annual sum of
US$ X million for the next 100 years – one year
for each year of denial. The proceeds were to be
split into two equal halves. One half would be
paid to a UN-sponsored fund that would help
destitute Armenians around the world and the
other half would also be paid in US dollars into
a Turkish-domiciled bank to help with the
rehabilitation of historic Armenian churches,
monasteries and monuments in Anatolia. Parts
of these funds were derived from funds that
were previously allocated to public relations
firms and advocates to deny the genocide.

As part of an overall settlement, the Nagorno-
Karabakh issue was also resolved. Armenia
retained South Karabakh and the Lachin
corridor and ceded Northern Karabakh and the
rest of Azeri lands to Azerbaijan.

In exchange for this and other crucial provisos,
the Armenian Diaspora and the Republic of
Armenia renounced all claims to its 3,000-year-
old historic Anatolian homeland, but retained
legal rights to historic and religious sites and
buildings across all Turkia.

This was just the beginning. In 2015 President X
also passed through the parliament laws that

affected the south-eastern provinces, with large Kurdish minorities. Kurdish became the second legal language in these territories: in public buildings and places, public communications such as radio and television and in public networks. By 2020, Turkey encouraged the formation of the state of Kurdistan – the historic homeland of the Kurds, incorporating lands not just from south-eastern Turkia, but also from northern Iraq and northern Iran. Neither Iran nor Iraq contested. Iran even allowed Azerbaijan to enhance its territory by amalgamating the Azeri population and lands in northern Iran.

Strange as that may seem to us today, the reason was pure economics. National governments had learnt the moral that "less is more". Governments soon realized that if their countries were to progress, they were compelled to invest in their people and in their land. If they did not intend to invest in that part of the country, they were better off devolving it. The less territory a country had, the less their costs, which meant there was more money left over.

Corruption, which until now was a highly-rewarded and acceptable way of Turkish life, was swiftly eradicated, through strict laws and high profile jail sentences. Numerous earthquakes had also helped galvanize Turkish public opinion. Those paying bribes and those accepting bribes were equally guilty and were punished swiftly and severely. Let's now look at the social catalysts.

Social catalysts

One of the primary social catalysts was the internet. With the advent and proliferation of the internet 30 years ago, it became extremely difficult to keep secrets: there was always someone who wanted to shed light in dark corners. Why? Because the rewards for exposing new stories were very high and the cost was almost zero. It was not a bad thing, unless you were afraid of what the light would show. As time went by, this increased exponentially. Turkia could not stop it: it spread like a virus.

Turkia had two choices. The first choice was that it could keep its people illiterate and control access to the internet; the results were obvious. The entrepreneurial individuals of the business community would emigrate and the Turkish economy would not only suffer, but very likely would never recover. The second choice was to take advantage of the inevitability of an open society with open communications and transparency. Global and international business organizations were compelled to be transparent. They could not say one thing to employees and another to customers. The truth would invariably come out in Internet chat rooms, books, newspapers, magazines and radio and television programs. Witness the traumas business organizations suffered as a result of the negative publicity they received when damning reports revealed bad practices. Remember how it all started with Nike and the story that it indirectly managed sweat shops or slave shops in the Far East. The result was always a disaster because the discredited organization's share price invariably took a serious dive. These corporations all live in the same ecosystem and they play by the same rules. With national governments, the story remains unchanged.

So how did Turks deal with this negative image? Initially, they denied, denied and denied it. Then they slowly responded by making out that the victims were in fact nothing more than enemies of war and later a civil war. Back in the 1980s, its public relations advocates, smelling long-term opportunity for profits, encouraged them to spend large sums of monies on creating Turkish chairs at leading universities in the US.

Some succeeded, but most failed, for a number of reasons. One reason that became self-evident was that the Turks had started a campaign to rewrite history. The generous Turkish endowments to US universities had strings attached and for that reason, once revealed, the self-respecting US universities were compelled to refuse. This was a time to change strategy.

There is a Turkish saying that says when the winds (of change) are blowing fiercely, a tree must bend so that it does not break. So too with Turkia: it was compelled, out of self-interest, to become more flexible so as not to break. For Turkia to prepare its people for this new century, it was compelled to educate its people to enable them to compete in a global marketplace. Back in 2002, Turkia did not have an all-round positive image abroad. This was in large part thanks to the image that Turkia impressed on the deported Armenians, who had since 1915 dispersed to all corners of the world. They carried with them memories that did not show Turkey in good light. They were not fabricating malicious rumors: they carried their own truth. In the face of almost 100 years of Turkish denial of the Armenian genocide, Armenians were left with no option but to ensure that every nation, every state, every province, every city, memorializes their pain and loss – so their story could never be wiped from history of mankind. They were protecting their own truth. This needed to change. Turkia could not afford to become poorer and poorer, because of misplaced pride. Reconciliation was no longer an option that could be delayed.

One social catalyst burst open in the culinary and gastronomy arena. Turks are awakening from the monolithic nation-state to the memory of their pluralistic past. Back in 2002, *The Wall Street Journal Europe* reported on an Ottoman restaurant called "Zarifi", offering neo-Ottoman cuisine, which opened up in Pera, a Bohemian district in Istanbul, not far from Istiklal Street. Sophisticated Istanbul residents – media faces, soccer stars and politicians – flocked to taste the long-forgotten multi-ethnic and imperial Ottoman dishes. Arabic food is served alongside Armenian, Balkan, Byzantine-Greek, Hungarian, Jewish and Russian dishes.

The journal reported the following assortments of Ottoman cuisine. *Muhammara* – an Arabic dip of crushed angry-red peppers, walnut meal, cheese and spices – was served alongside *komshuyani* – a Jewish tagine of stewed lamb, quince, plums and onions. A rare Armenian dish called *topik* "astonished the palate" – a mildly spiced, baked chick-pea flour croquette stuffed with minced lamb, raisins, mint and onions sautéed with tahini. Byzantine-Greek *sahanikis* – casseroles of single portion lamb, cheese or seafood – "endured in the taste memory". The Hungarian honeyed eggplant was simply "an undreamt-of revelation".

Of the desserts, the one new-found treasure hailed from the Aegean: a mélange of stewed plums, quince pears and the like. But what was not covered are the bigger surprises to be found in the obscure history of the traditional Ottoman desserts, such as the common *baklava*. The word originates from the Armenian word *baki-helva* meaning Lenten sweets. In the distant past, Armenian families would prepare trays of 40 *baki-helva* pieces, one for each of the 40 days of Lent. When Armenian nobles presented the dessert to the Sultan in Constantinople, he liked it so much that it became an Imperial Ottoman dessert. Since 2002, Ottoman restaurants gradually opened in many cities across Europe and North America.

The Ottoman Empire had its glorious zenith and its shameful downfall. Over time, Turks realized that they had to embrace their past, if they were

The future: I have a dream 81

to look to the future with confidence. They realized that they themselves were sending a confused message not just to the world at large, but to their own people. If they were proud to celebrate their glorious past, such as the 1987 Exhibition of the 500th Anniversary of Suleiman the Magnificent, the 1992 Splendors of the Ottoman Sultans and the 2000 Palace of Gold and Light: Treasures from Topkapi, they also needed to confront and embrace the ghosts of their past, put them to rest and move on. The double-talk of being proud of the Ottomans one minute and then back-tracking when it wasn't suitable, left a question mark. The creation of an artificial legalistic divide between Ottoman Turkey and post-1923 Turkey is a temporary stop gap: it could never stand the course of time. Checkmate is the word when your opponent runs out of moves in chess and he has nowhere to go. The word checkmate originates from the Persian, *Shah Mat,* which means "The King – or Sultan – is dead". Let a new game begin.

Other social catalysts included the areas of education, tourism, and religion. Once again, President X took the helm and steered Turkia through the choppy waters of change.

Education focused on teaching skills and

literacy. The young and unemployed from the Europe Union came on one- and two-year shifts to teach English, German, French and Spanish to the Turks, and although they were not paid very much, their food and lodgings were covered and they gained more than just a teaching experience.

Tourism flourished too, as Armenians, feeling safe and secure that Turkia was a reformed country, visited it frequently, bringing with them trade and tourism. Even the Greeks started visiting Turkia in large numbers, also looking for the remnants of their once-lost cultural heritage. Turkia's Ministry of Tourism and Culture was promoted by Armenians and Greeks in the West and around the world. Hotel and car rental franchises sprung like mushrooms, all over Anatolia. Tour operators could not satisfy demand. There was just not enough available accommodation in the first few years. As the money generated by tourism flowed through the rest of the economy, both Turkia and Armenia prospered.

In retrospect, one of the few remaining benefits of Atatürk's legacy was the separation of religion and state. As a result, religion was in essence a private affair. This had not really

The future: I have a dream 83

filtered down the population, which was predominantly Muslim. Things changed significantly after the September 11, 2001 terrorist attack on America. First regional governments worked together and terrorism was significantly eradicated across the world. Second, the creation of a sovereign Palestinian state was formally approved by a 2005 treaty in which all Arab states not only accepted Israel's right to exist but declared they would openly denounce any form of terrorism. As a result of this historic step, the Muslim religion returned to a tolerant state, where it respected other religions and allowed other religions to be practiced in their lands. Let's now look at the economic catalysts.

Economic catalysts

The combined political and social catalysts opened up a whole new world of economic possibilities. Avenues and routes that were closed or non-existent were now feasible. The unthinkable became possible.

With peace secured in the region and guaranteed by all regional powers, Russian oil and gas was piped to the world from three points. First, Russia's Siberian oil was piped under the Siberian snow across the Bering Straits, Alaska, and western Canada into the United States. Second, oil and gas was piped through Chechnya, Georgia and Armenia to Iran's port of Abadan on the Persian Gulf. Third, Azerbaijan's oil was piped through both Georgia and Armenia to Turkia's Mediterranean ports of Ceyhan.

Azerbaijan's detached province of Nakhichevan, which lies huddled between Turkia and Armenia, was an issue that irked Azerbaijan. These partitions were a poisonous legacy of Stalin, whose aim was to keep these tribes divided and at each others' throats. This situation was resolved in the course of the peace negotiations and treaties that ensued, to the satisfaction of both Armenia and Azerbaijan: a flyover highway was constructed over Armenian airspace that joined the non-contiguous province to its sister provinces. In exchange, Azeri oil and gas traversed Armenia and helped grow its treasury.

With its new access to the Black Sea, Armenia built a new port not far from the old town of Hopa: a new port that dispatched exports of Armenian goods to the world outside and received imports from the rest of the world. It took two years to build a new four-lane 300 kilometer highway to link this new port to Gyumri, Armenia's second largest city, via a highway that passed near Artvin, Ardahan and Kars.

Diaspora Armenians engaged not only in the physical building of Armenia, but in the building of skills and services of its population. Many young Armenian entrepreneurs from North America, Europe, the Middle East and Australia visited Armenia for periods ranging from two months to two years. They were there not just to get experience and learn about their culture, but also to give something back to their native country. Engineers, physicists, chemists, doctors, lawyers, journalists, academics, artists, painters, dancers, singers and musicians – all contributed and learnt from this exceptional experience.

Turkia's Ministry of Tourism and Culture in conjunction with the Genocide Reparations Council created a master program of rehabilitating and unearthing ancient and holy Armenian sites in Anatolia. Turks and Armenians worked together for their mutual benefit. With American-Armenian funds, a strategy was devised to locate Holiday Inn hotels and Alamo car rentals franchises in all the major centers such as Van, Bitlis, Erzerum, Sivas, Kayseri, Malatya, Trabzon, Urfa and Aintab, where a deluge of tourists of Armenian origin descended each month of the year. Tour operators focused on holiday packages that combined cultural aspects and beach vacations on Turkia's Mediterranean coast.

The unprecedented economic boom that had detonated all over Anatolia had left the business community in Istanbul and the political class in Ankara in a state of wonderment. Hotels, resorts, museums, restaurants and shops were under construction everywhere. A massive influx of investment monies from the US and EU was drip-feeding into Turkia's economy. In the cafes and bars, there was one question that kept surfacing over and over again: "why had no one thought about this before?"

Conclusion

In the past, although Turkia's nationalistic stance had fostered a strong sense of national unity, it had also created a certain xenophobic streak in the Turkish nation. Turkish foreign policy in the past aided and abetted this feeling.

The republic, born in blood-letting, saw nothing but dangers on all its borders. There was a common belief among Turks that they do not have friends: their republic only has interests. It could only rely on the raw and steely strength of its armed forces. They soon realized that if you didn't believe in friendship – be it political, economic or social – and you didn't practice the art of making friends, then it was not unreasonable to discover why you didn't have any friends. The first rule of making friends was, and still is, to be one.

When a friend does something bad, the solution is simply to say they are sorry. For many, saying sorry is easy, but it is the cost of saying sorry that concerns them. For Turkia, the problem was not just the cost: even saying sorry was a problem. Why? Because Turkia's national pride, on which so much had been built, covered and invested, would be crushed, they thought. The reality, of course, was different. What was the value of Turkish national pride, when it was based on covering up historical truths? Shouldn't national pride be genuine and truthful? Shouldn't Turkish national pride be strong enough to admit that in the process of creating their republic out of the rubble of the Ottoman Empire, their leaders committed many evil crimes against other peoples?

In 1915, Cain once again killed Abel. In that same year, the leaders of the larger and more powerful Turkish nation killed their smaller, younger and weaker brother: the Armenian nation. Where was the Turkish national pride in the cowardly arrest of all able-bodied Armenian men and then butchering them? Where was the Turkish national pride when brigands and convicts were encouraged to rape and mutilate defenseless Armenian women and children? Where was the Turkish national pride in stealing the land, goods and possessions that belonged to others? If a nation's pride were to be measured like you measure praise for an achievement – then the praise of others would mean the most. After all what use is self-praise? So, by separating the good elements of the Republic's foundation from the bad elements, Turkish national pride could be salvaged. Turkia could redeem itself, where Cain could not.

There is a saying in English that "pride comes before a fall". This national pride of Turkia was such that it has contributed greatly to its poverty and suffering. Remember Cain: "You are banished from the ground, which has opened its mouth to receive your brother's blood from your

The future: I have a dream 89

hand. When you try to cultivate the ground, it will no longer yield its best for you." So why was Turkia's soil and toil lacking growth? Because their forefathers cleansed the soil of the ingredients that nourished the soil of productivity: Armenians, Greeks and other Christians. So, how could Turkia's soil become more productive? It needed to replenish the land with the missing ingredients. Was it not better to have a share in a land that is prospering and rich than entirely own a land that is infertile and poor?

One a wet day in Sepember 2005, before all these developments took place, a man with a Turkish-sounding name phoned me. He said he was in London for a few days and wanted to speak to me about this book. When I pressed him as to why he wanted to see me specifically, he relented: "I am the great-grandson of the Süleyman Nejmi Bey – the one you mentioned in your book – and I would like to meet with you." We have met and talked many times since then. A decade later, this man would become the Chief-of-Staff to the future President X.

This is just a dream. Many are afraid to dream

because it exposes them to ridicule. People therefore dream but do not share their dream and it dies with them. You might say my dream is sad and pathetic. You might even say my dream is the dream of a sad and pathetic man. I would defend your right to say that. I would also challenge you to come up with your own dream. It's quite possible that your dream may unlock the doors to reconciliation between Armenians and Turks. I could then hold the honor that my book contributed to hatching your dream. It is, after all, thanks to dreamers that mankind has made the immense progress over the last millennia. Without dreamers, we would still be living in caves. I leave you with this quote to ponder:

"You see things; and you say Why? But I dream things that never were; and I say Why not?"
George Bernard Shaw

Appendices

Appendix A

The Public Record Office in Richmond, Surrey, UK, provided 10 pages of copy documents relating to charges against Suleiman Nedjmi Bey. The 8th page is a translation from the French. These documents were the result of witness accounts assembled against Suleiman Nedjmi Bey while the British held him prisoner on the island of Malta, awaiting trial on charges of massacring Armenians. Nedjmi Bey was among 144 top-ranking Ottoman officers interned in Malta by the British on similar charges.

Appendix B

Oberlin College Archives, in Oberlin, Ohio, provided documents, letters and news articles from the student alumni file of Mary Louise Graffam. Among them was this obituary dated 8 September 1921.

Appendix C

Miss Mary Louise Graffam wrote this letter from Malatia to a correspondent in Constantinople (Istanbul), which Boston's *Missionary Herald* later published in December 1915. This same letter was included by Viscount James Bryce and Arnold Toynbee in their British Parliamentary blue book series, *The Treatment of the Armenians in the Ottoman Empire 1915–1916*, recently republished by Gomidas Institute, Princeton, New Jersey.

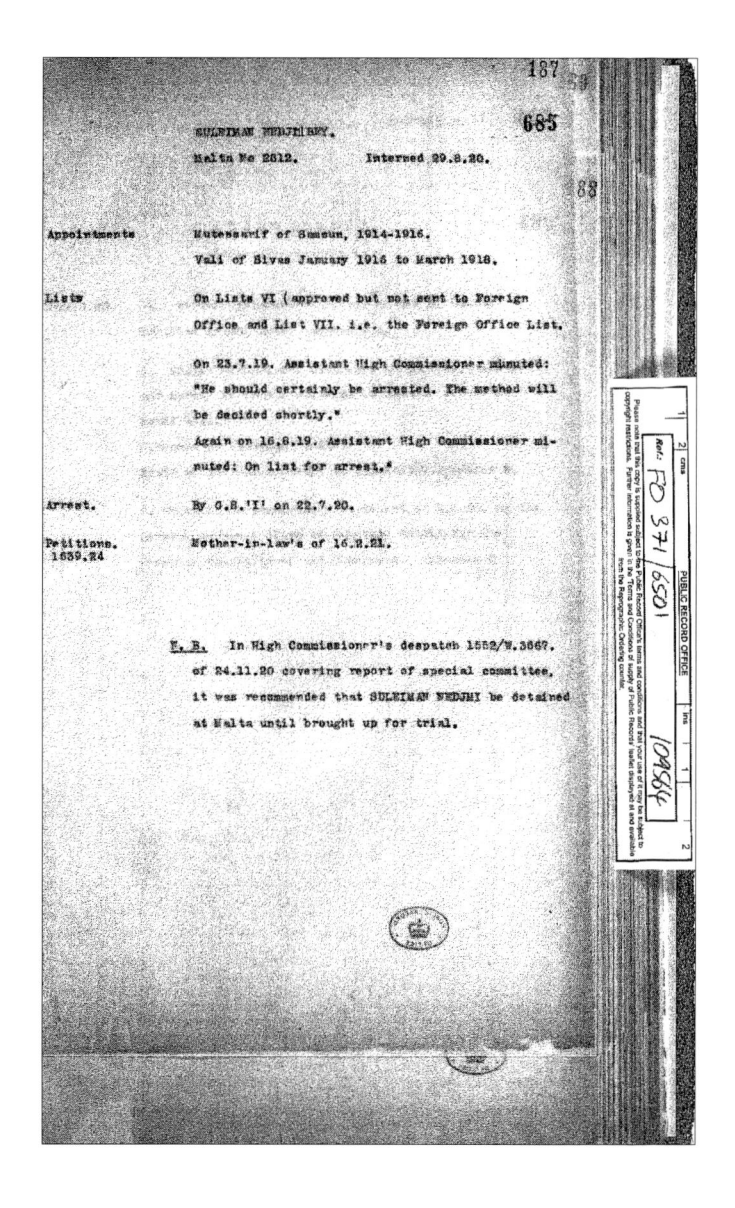

SULEIMAN NEDJMI BEY.

Malta No 2812.   Interned 29.8.20.

Appointments Mutessarif of Samsun, 1914-1916.
Vali of Sivas January 1916 to March 1918.

Lists On Lists VI (approved but not sent to Foreign Office and List VII. i.e. the Foreign Office List.

On 23.7.19. Assistant High Commissioner minuted: "He should certainly be arrested. The method will be decided shortly."

Again on 16.8.19. Assistant High Commissioner minuted: On list for arrest."

Arrest. By C.S.'I' on 22.7.20.

Petitions. Mother-in-law's of 16.2.21.
1839.24

N. B. In High Commissioner's despatch 1552/W.3667. of 24.11.20 covering report of special committee, it was recommended that SULEIMAN NEDJMI be detained at Malta until brought up for trial.

APPENDIX A.

ACCUSATIONS.

8029.A.20   A. Signed statement of 1.7.19/murder of Hampar Zakarian in May 1915. Appendix A.

B. Krikor Nichanian's statement of 28.7.20. Torture and murder of Hampar Zakarian in Samsoun prison in April 1915.
Massacre of Tatarian family.
Death of the naked martyr at Tchakalli. Appendix B.

C. Hagop N. Gueuvchanian's statement of 5.8.20. on the general responsibility of SULEIMAN NEDJMI for the Armenian deportations and massacres. Appendix C.

189

APPENDIX A.   687

Extract from a statement signed by a large number of
Armenians of Samsoun; dated 1.7.19 and sent to the High
Commission by the Armenian Committee of Samsoun.

N.B. Father Karikin Chinikdjian, the Armenian priest
of Samsoun in May 1915 has since been massacred.

Hampar Zakarian was a poor Armenian (?) maker
and without any cause like the other Armenians of the
city has been taken into prison. In the prison he has
been tried to make him confess the imaginary secretes
of the Armenian Committees. He has refused to calumniate
any one. Fedjmi Bey (Mutessarif) has ordered to strip
and torture him by red hot irons. This could not be du-
rated long, so on 7th May 1915 on fridays midnight, at
3 o'clock a.m. an armed troop of Turkish gendarmeries have
called the named Armenian priest Father Karekin Chinikdjian
out of his house without telling him the cause and forced
him to follow them. They have leaded him to the Armenian
cemetery, there the Father has found a covered coffin near
to a diged grave. They have ordered him to bury the unknown
dead. The priest in the service when has opened the covering of the coffin, to put a grasp of soil in it, (that
is an ecclesiastical rule), with horror has seen that
the unknown dead is Hampar Zakarian and his body is wholly
tortured. Next morning every Armenian heard this sad
new in detail tolled by the priest and Turkish gendarmeries.
Forty days Turkish gendarmeries continuely day and night
have kept sentinel on the grave not to leave to any body to
approach to the grave and to hasten the putrifaction have
put lime every day on the grave (they believe that lime
does it):-

APPENDIX B.

TEMOIGNAGE D'UN ARMENIEN DE SAMSOUN SUR LE CAS DU CRIMINEL B.Y. MUTESSARIF de SAMSOUN

b. Beilegman Vedjmi Bey has declared to Armenians that whoever that turns Mohammedan will be safed. 500 Armenians have done it. He has send some of them to Baffra other to Fhatsa, after keeping them there about two weaks, has called them back and told that they will reside at Kavak but after sending them there has given order to the meudir of Kavak not to keep them there but send soon to Sivas into the had of Mozmber Bey (The Vali of Sivas) to be massacred by the organised troops of the later and in order that no armenian whether has become Mohammedan or not to succeed to remain in Kavak has send Latif Bey the commander of gendarmery to pursue them and fulfil his desires:

c. There was an order from Constantinople that if there were Armenians who were taken into military service their families should be spared, but VEDJMI Bey in spite to this order has ordered to exile even this kind armenian families

d. During deportation of Armenians from Samsoun Beileyman VEDJMI Bey has tried by every means not to spare even to pregnant women and sicks and ecclesiastics. Has hired heralds and told them to cry in the streets that if anybody whether Mohammedan or Greek that dares to keep and safe an Armenian, should be judged and hanged. If today there are armenians that in spite of such severe execution are saved that is by a miracle and every survived armenian has its own history of horror, and to be true we must add that the Greek prelate of Samsoun has done his best for the Armenians to help them in any way.

Sir, after leaving the case to Your Highness, we expect soon to see the judgment and the punishment of Beileyman VEDJMI BEY.

APPENDIX B.

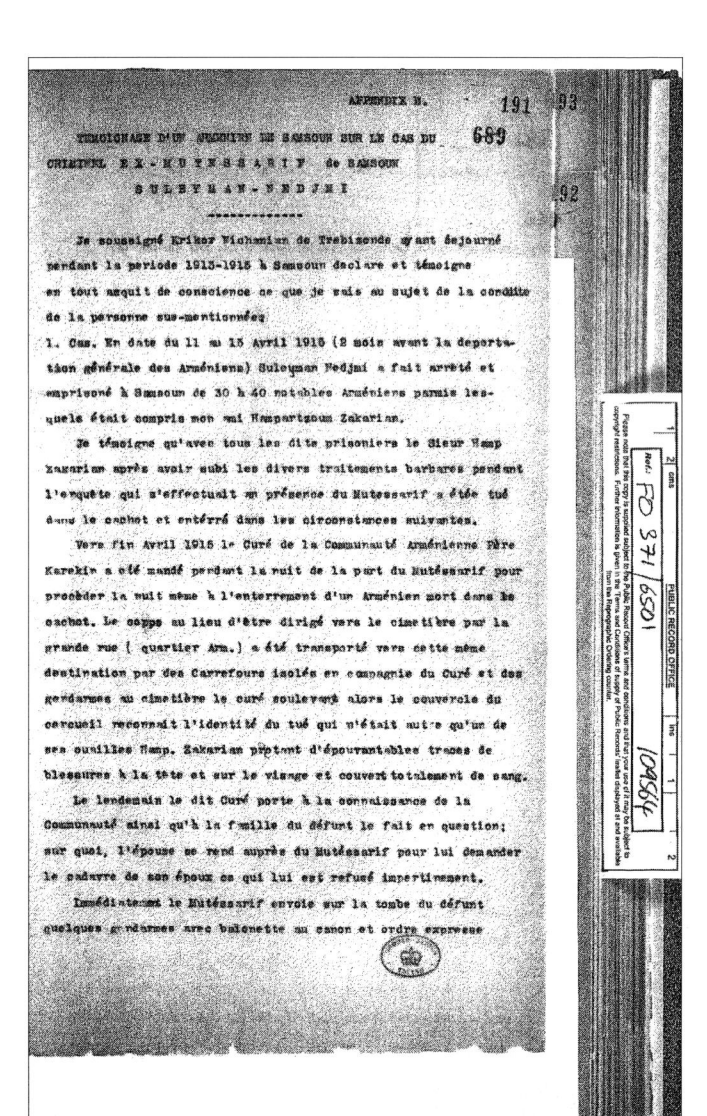

TÉMOIGNAGE D'UN JUCOMIER DE SAMSOUN SUR LE CAS DU
CRIMINEL EX-MUTESSARIF de SAMSOUN
SULEYMAN-FEDJMI

Je soussigné Krikor Vichmian de Trebizonde ayant séjourné pendant la période 1913-1915 à Samsoun déclare et témoigne en tout acquit de conscience ce que je sais au sujet de la conduite de la personne sus-mentionnée.

1. Cas. En date du 11 au 13 Avril 1915 (2 mois avant la déportation générale des Arméniens) Suleyman Fedjmi a fait arrêter et emprisonner à Samsoun de 30 à 40 notables Arméniens parmis lesquels était compris mon ami Hampartzoum Zakarian.

Je témoigne qu'avec tous les dits prisoniers le Sieur Hamp Zakarian après avoir subi les divers traitements barbares pendant l'enquête qui s'effectuait en présence du Mutéssarif a été tué dans le cachot et enterré dans les circonstances suivantes.

Vers fin Avril 1915 le Curé de la Communauté Arménienne Père Karekin a été mandé pendant la nuit de la part du Mutéssarif pour procéder la nuit même à l'enterrement d'un Arménien mort dans le cachot. Le corps au lieu d'être dirigé vers le cimetière par la grande rue (quartier Arm.) a été transporté vers cette même destination par des Carrefours isolés en compagnie du Curé et des gendarmes au cimetière le curé soulevant alors le couvercle du cercueil reconnait l'identité du tué qui n'était autre qu'un de ses ouailles Hamp. Zakarian prtant d'épouvantables traces de blessures à la tête et sur le visage et couvert totalement de sang.

Le lendemain le dit Curé porte à la connaissance de la Communauté ainsi qu'à la famille du défunt le fait en question; sur quoi, l'épouse se rend auprès du Mutéssarif pour lui demander le cadavre de son époux ce qui lui est refusé impertinemment.

Immédiatement le Mutéssarif envoie sur la tombe du défunt quelques gendarmes avec baïonette au canon et ordre expresse

Appendix A

d'y monter une garde rigoureuse, quelques semaines plus tard on ne sait par quelle mentalité on déterre le dit cadavre conformément aux instructions du Mutéssarif et on le brûle.

2. Cas. En date du 21 Juin 1915 alors que la deportation générale avait eu lieu et que moi et ma famille nous séjournions à Samson en qualité d'Islam que nous avions embrassé antérieurement un de nos amis Mr Bédros Tatarian osché jusqu' à lors chez lui; avec toute sa famille venant chez moi me prit d'intercéder auprès du Mutéssarif dont j'étais connu, afin de les faire admettre aussi à accepter l'Islamisme.

Le Mutéssarif après avoir acquiescer à notre demande, transmet aussitôt après notre départ de chez lui les instructions nécessaires auprès de qui de doit afin d'opérer à l'arrestation et à la deportation immédiate de son ami avec toute sa famille ordre, qui fut exécuté immédiatement; Depuis lors on n'a aucune nouvelle sur leur sort.

Déporté au bourg d'Alatchem où je demeurai/qualifié en Islam en date du 16 Juillet 1915 on m'a fait reintégré Samsoun d'où j'ai été de nouveau deporté avec ma famille vers une direction inconnue.

Après une demie heure de parcours, nous avons constaté qu'une personne toute nue les mains liés au dos faisait suite pédestrement à notre convoi en voiture, les gendarmes qui nous accompagnaient lui criaient à la face impertinement (Hayéf Obinavur Yétich) et le soumettaient à une bastonnade régulière, d'ailleurs le corps du Martyr était empreinte de nombreuses blessures qu'il portait déjà et se trouvait dans un état épouvantable.

Après une marche d'une journée alors que nous étions a peine arrivés à Tchakalli accompagnés toujours du Martyr nu, qui suivait continuellement à pied notre convoi nous avons voulu intercéder en faveur du Martyr auprès des gendarmes qui l'accompagnaient afin d'adoucir quelques peu leur mauvais traitement envers le demi-mort; pour toute réponse ils nous ont déclaré arrogamment qu'ils avaient reçu du mutéssarif des ordres formels pour éliminer la personne en question sur quoi les derniers coups de cravache ont plu sur le pauvre moribon qui a rendu devant nous son dernier soupir.

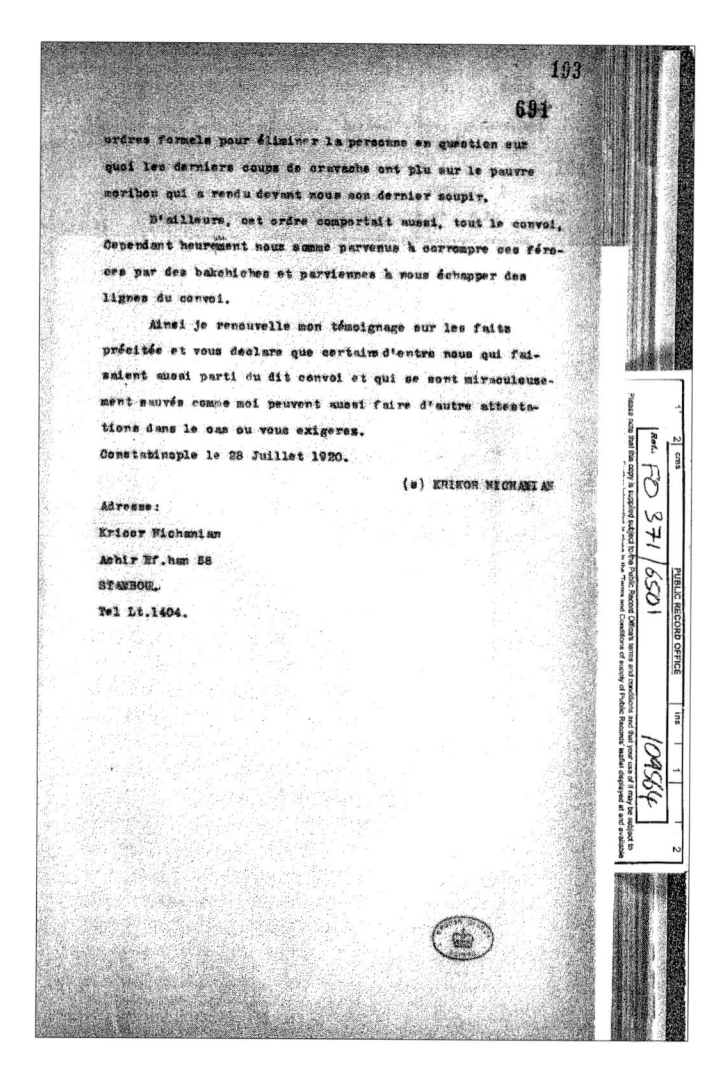

D'ailleurs, cet ordre comportait aussi, tout le convoi. Cependant heureusement nous sommes parvenus à corrompre ces féroces par des bakchiches et parviennes à nous échapper des lignes du convoi.

Ainsi je renouvelle mon témoignage sur les faits précités et vous declare que certains d'entre nous qui faisaient aussi parti du dit convoi et qui se sont miraculeusement sauvés comme moi peuvent aussi faire d'autre attestations dans le cas ou vous exigerez.

Constantinople le 28 Juillet 1920.

(s) KRIKOR NICHANIAN

Adresse:

Kricor Nichanian
Achir Ef. han 58
STAMBOUL
Tel Lt.1404.

miracle and every survi_____ (sic) Armenian has its (sic) own history of horror, and to t____ we must add that the Greek prelate of Samsun has done his best for the Armenians to help them in any way.

Sir, after leaving the case to Your Highness, we expect soon to see the judgement and punishment of Suleiman Nedjmi Bey.

APPENDIX B

TESTIMONY OF AN ARMENIAN FROM SAMSUN IN THE CASE OF EX-MUTESSARIF OF SAMSUN SULEIMAN NEDJMI

I, the undersigned Krikor Nishanian of Trebizond, resided at Samsun during the period 1913-1915 and declare and give witness herto to that which I know in relation to the above-mentioned person:

1/ Between the 11th and 15th April 1915 (two months before the general deportations of Armenians), Suleiman Nedjmi arrested and imprisoned at Samsun 30 to 40 Armenian notables, among whom was my friend Hampartzoum Zakarian.

I confirm that together with other prisoners Hampartzoum Zakarian - having survived barbaric treatment during the interrogation before the Mutessarif - was murdered in the dungeon in the following circumstances:

Towards the end of April 1915, the priest of the Armenian community, Father Karekin, was summoned during the night by the Mutessarif to direct the interment of an Armenian who had died in the dungeon. Instead of being directed to the Armenian cemetery via the main street, the body was taken down lonely back streets escorted by the Father and some Gendarmes, and when the Priest lifted the lid of the tomb he recognized his parishioner Hampartzoum Zakarian who had suffered the most terrible traces of wounds on head and face and was totally covered in blood.

The next day the Priest brought this t____ attention of the community as well as to the family of t__ dead person, at which the wife went to the Mutessarif to ask for the body of her husband, which was rudely refused.

The Mutessarif immediately instructed some Gendarmes to maintain careful watch over the tomb with fixed bayonetss. Some weeks later the corpse was removed on the instructions of the Mutessarif, and burned.

2/ On 21 June 1915 when the general deportation had already been launched my family and I were resident at Samsun as Muslims, which we had had to convert to, a friend of mine, Mr. Bedros Tatarian who was in hiding with his family asked me to intercede on their behalf with the Mutessarif whom I knew, to discover if they too could convert to Islam.

After having agreed to this request, the Mutessarif issued the necessary instructions for the immediate arrest and deportation of my friend with his entire family, and these instructions were carried out immediately. Since that moment we have had no news whatever of them.

I was deported to Alatchem, where I lived as a Muslim from 16 July 1915, then I was brought back to Samsun, whence once again I was deported to an unknown destination.

Half an hour en route we noticed a totally naked person with hands tied following our convoy on foot. The Gendarmes who escorted us screamed continually at (Hayde Giavour Yetish) and beat him regularly; his body was covered with numerous wounds and he was in terrible state.

After an entire day's march we were almost at Chakalli continuously in the company of this naked martyr who tried to keep up with the convoy, we attempted to intercede on his behalf with the guards to try to lighten his load. All they did was reply arrogantly that they had received formal orders from the Mutessarif about the person in question. The last assaults with the riding whip finally brought about the last breath of this unfortunate.

This order applied to the entire convoy. Fortunately for us we were able to escape from the lines of the convoy.

APPENDIX C.

STATEMENT MADE AT THE HIGH COMMISSION ON 5.8.20
BY HAGOP GUFUVCHENIAN, COMMISSION AGENT OF SAMSUN; NOW OF
KUTCHUK TURKIA HAN, CHEZ BALUKDJIAN FRERES STAMBOUL.

I left Samsun 3 months ago.

I know SULEIMAN NEDJMI personally. He was Mutassarif from 1914 to 1916 when he became Vali of Sivas. He left Samsun just before the arrival of Refet Pasha and the Beginning of the Greek deportations.

In June 1915 the deportation of Armenians began from Samsun. I myself was protected by the Persian consul, but my family consisting of 10 people was deported into Sivas vilayet and massacred between Amassia and Tokat with the knowledge and consent of SULEIMAN NEDJMI at the end of June 1915.

Again in September 1915, I was deported together with 22 Armenian men, women and children, by direct order of NEDJMI. I myself escaped from the convoy but all the remainder were murdered just south of Amassia.

SULEIMAN NEDJMI knew as well as every other person in Samsun, what was to be the fate of all Armenian deportees.

Within a week of the first deportations every Armenian knew that deportation was an euphemism for massacre. The Mutessarif of course knew this better even than we did. He had placards put up about the town warning all greeks against harbouring Armenians under pain of death by hanging. There were no wholesale massacres of Armenians within the boundaries of the sandjak. The massacres began just south of Kavak on the Sivas boundary.

Some 5 or 6 Armenian intellectuals of Samsun were arrested in May 1915 and thrown into prison. In 1916 NEDJMI ordered the then President of the Court Martial Osman Senayi Bey to condemn these men, but he refused saying there was no evidence against them. For this NEDJMI dismissed him and sent to Constantinople. Before leaving Osman Senpeti came to say goodbye to the Persian Consul where I was hidden and told him the circumstances of his dismissal. Nazim, the President of the Recruiting office was a member of the Court Martial. Though Nazim had full authority to do what he liked he was never President of the Court Martial Nazim was protected by Vehib Pasha. For the Greek atrocities I look upon Refet Pasha as undoubtedly chiefly responsible. Later Vehif Pasha dismissed Refet Pasha.

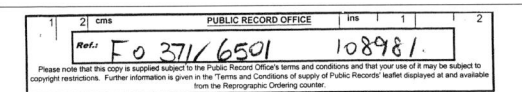

For practical purposes power passed into the hands of the Military after the occupation of Trebizond by the Russians.

Witness can corroborate in regard to murder of Hampar Zakarian by order of SULEIMAN FEDJMI; also in regard to the Tartarian family (502(/A/20).

N.B. An intelligent witness.

Protector of the Poor in Sivas
Mary Louise Graffam
1871-1921

"Mary Graffam has finished her course," exclaimed one of the American Board staff as he read a cable message received on Aug. 25. It said, "Seven days after operation Graffam died Sivas, Aug. 17." That was all. The Board does not know, yet, any details of the events in Sivas which culminated on Aug. 17. But the fitting words flashed to mind, "The time of my departure is come. I have fought the good fight. I have finished the course. I have kept the faith."

Sept. 8, 1921

but she had it, as was very soon proven when German officers and doctors made their appearance in Sivas and Miss Graffam was able to consult, confer and often command in that tongue.

Readers of *The Congregationalist* have already heard of the more sensational events since 1914 in which Miss Graffam was concerned; how going to the front at Erzroom when the Russians and Turks were clashing, she went with an American nurse way up under fire in the vain attempt to rescue the nurse's husband, dying of typhus. In Erzroom, with no professional training, she was made matron and head nurse of a Red Crescent hospital for wounded officers. Here she confirmed her knowledge of Turkish! When she could leave Erzroom she started back, across the mountains toward Sivas and her companion, a Swiss nurse, died of typhus. Miss Graffam knew she would herself probably come down with it, but she sent word to Sivas that they need not send for her, because there would be two days of consciousness if she was attacked and she would let them know then!

That was early in 1915. Then began the Deportations. She set forth with "her people"— about 3,000 who were connected with the mission. The story of that journey can never be fully told—of the robbery, hunger, thirst, discase, the kidnapping, murder—and all under a blistering July sun across the dusty plains of Asia Minor. When they came to Malatia the Turks told Miss Graffam she could go no further. "I remained in Malatia three weeks. If anything could be a counterpart of the worst description of Hell, that place was Malatia."

She got back to Sivas in time to see more German consuls and military officers. But in May, 1916, the mission buildings were seized and all Americans except Miss Graffam and Miss Fowle were evicted. These two women, both familiar with Turkish character and language, were assigned to a small house to care for the orphanages which were already crowded and growing. The refugees from the East, Moslems, Greeks and Russians among them, began to crowd into Sivas over the roads from the South and East. They came to the two Americans, who could have used many times the amount of money and medicine they had in caring for this new multitude of helpless, hopeless humanity. In the midst of these demands Miss Fowle died of typhus.

That left Mary Graffam the only human refuge for thousands and tens of thousands. After Miss Fowle's death Miss Graffam made up her mind that she would herself certainly suffer death at the hands of the Turks, for she was persecuted and annoyed constantly. She was tried for treason on one occasion. But she determined to sell her life as dearly as possible and, having accepted death, she lost all fear of it and went on with her plans regardless of crowding evils. The Turks could not understand such an attitude and became afraid of her!

She organized industrial work: started a knitting factory "working for the government," if any one inquired, leased a farm from German authorities, a farm alleged to have been German crown property, but valuable for its water power, which Miss Graffam applied to operate gristmills and for irrigating the various crops she set her refugees to cultivating.

By the time the Near East relief workers arrived after the Armistice, she had shops for carpentry, tailoring, weaving, shoemaking and blacksmith's work; 1,100 orphans in various institutions; five gristmills and various farms outside the city.

Miss Mary L. Graffam

Appendix B

Born in Monson, Me., May 11, 1871, Mary Louise Graffam embarked for Turkey in August, 1901, just twenty years before the time of her going on. Although a graduate of Oberlin College she lived for some time in Massachusetts and was a member of the South Church in Andover.

Very soon after she reached Turkey, Miss Graffam's name appeared as Principal of the Girls' School in Sivas and presently it was on the staff of the Teachers' College, the promising normal school in the city. Up to the time of her first furlough, her activities increased and her knowledge of all kinds of mission and school work and of life among the people made a splendid preparation for the work to which she was going back so unconsciously.

"Acquisition of new languages was sport for Miss Graffam," writes Miss Ethel Hubbard in her brief but thrilling book, *Lone Sentinels in the Near East*, and she goes on: "Less than a year gave her ease and pungency in the Armenian speech, a summer in Geneva mobilized her French and four months of another year—a decisive and terrible year—gave her an opportune knowledge of Turkish. Regular teacher of algebra, geometry and Bible in the Girls' School, of trigonometry in Teachers' College, substitute teacher of any and all subjects no one else happened to want; church organist; mission treasurer; director of Y. M. C. A. relief work for widows; itinerant missionary traveling on horseback—a mode of travel she detested—to distant villages, sometimes through mountain blizzards and deep snows; frequent visitor in Turkish harems, a leading figure in social, musical and literary events—this intrepid, dominating, irrepressible personality was Mary Graffam in the years before the War."

We are not told where she acquired German, and more of the systematic deportation and killing. The Sivas men were all in prison. Those destined for death were put each day in a certain small building. They sent to beg Miss Graffam to come to take messages from them, to pray with them. "I went to the prison every day to say good-bye to them," she wrote. "I was half crazed; and yet I could not give in to it because refugees were beginning to come from other places."

Now the relief work began and here she tried far and did secure some help and influence from Major General Harbord, who was sent through Armenia in 1919, said that Miss Graffam had played a part in those years never equaled by any other woman in missionary chronicles.

Her visible presence has passed. Her work

MISS GRAFFAM AND WAR WORKERS IN SIVAS

Left to right, a German physician, Miss Foule, Miss Graffam, a German Army Officer

is going on. A Mary Graffam Memorial must some day rise in that wide land and at the hands of those differing races and kinds of people for whom she gave herself with such unstinted devotion and among whom she finished her course.

F. S. F.

78. SIVAS: LETTER WRITTEN FROM MALATIA BY MISS MARY L. GRAFFAM PRINCIPAL OF THE GIRLS' HIGH SCHOOL AT SIVAS, TO A CORRESPONDENT AT CONSTANTINOPLE; REPRINTED FROM THE BOSTON "MISSIONARY HERALD" DECEMBER, 1915

When we were ready to leave Sivas the Government gave forty-five ox-carts for the Protestant townspeople and eighty horses, but none at all for our pupils and teachers; so we bought ten ox-carts, two horse arabas, and five or six donkeys, and started out. In the company were all our teachers in the college, about twenty boys from the college and about thirty of the girls'-school. It was as a special favour to the Sivas people, who had not done anything revolutionary, that the Vali allowed the men who were not yet in prison to go with their families.

The first night we were so tired that we just ate a piece of bread and slept on the ground wherever we could find a place to spread a *yorgan* (blanket). It was after dark when we stopped, anyway. We were so near Sivas that the gendarmes protected us and no special harm was done; but the second night we began to see what was before us. The gendarmes would go ahead and have long conversations with the villagers, and then stand back and let them rob and trouble the people until we all began to scream, and then they would come and drive them away. *Yorgans* and rugs, and all such things, disappeared by the dozen, and donkeys were sure to be lost. Many had brought cows; but from the first day those were carried off, one by one, until not a single one remained.

We got accustomed to being robbed, but the third day a new fear took possession of us, and that was that the men were to be separated from us at Kangal. We passed there at noon and, apart from fear, nothing special happened. Our teacher from Mandjaluk there, with his mother and sisters. They had left the village with the rest of the women and children, and when they saw that the men were being taken off to be killed the teacher fled to another village, four hours away, where he was found by the police and brought safely with his family to Kangal, because the tchaoush who had taken them from Mandjaluk wanted his sister, found them confined in one room, went to the Kaïmakam and got an order for them all to come with us.

At Kangal some Armenians had become Mohammedans and had not left the village, but the others were all gone. The night before we had spent at Kazı Mahara, which was empty. They said that valley there full of corpses. At Kangal we also began to see exiles from Tokat. The sight was one to strike horror to any heart, they were a company of old women, who had been robbed of absolutely everything. At Tokat the Government had first imprisoned the men, and from the prison had taken them on the road. The preacher's wife was in the company, and told us the story. After the men had

---

Date unspecified

{?Mr. Peet}. {ORIGINAL. Copy of Mary L. Graffam to William Peet letter dated Malatia, 7 August, 1915 in Ambassador Morgenthau to Secretary of State communication dated 13 September 1915. NA/RG59/867.4016/187. —A.S.}

gone, they arrested the old women and the older brides, perhaps about thirty or thirty-five years old. There were very few young women or children. All the younger women and children were left in Tokat. Badvelli Avedis has seven children; one was with our schoolgirls and the other six remained in Tokat without father or mother to look after them. For three days these Tokat people had been without food, and after that had lived on the Sivas company, who had not yet lost much.

When we looked them we could not imagine that the sprinkling of that were with us would be allowed to remain. We did not long remain in doubt; the next day we heard that a special kaimakam had come to Hassan Tchelebi to separate the men, and it was with terror in our hearts that passed through that village about But encamped and ate our supper in peace, and even began to think that perhaps it was not so, when the Mudir came round with gendarmes and began to collect the men, saying that the Kaimakam wanted to write them and that they would be back soon.

The night passed, and only one man came back to tell the story of how every man was compelled to give up all his money, and all were taken to prison. The next morning they collected the men who had escaped the night before and extorted forty-five liras from our company, on the promise that they would give us gendarmes to protect us. One "company" is supposed to be from 1,000 to 3,000 persons. Ours was perhaps 2,000, and the greatest number of gendarmes would be five or six. In addition to these they sewed a red rag on the arm of a Kurdish villager and gave him a gun, and he had the right to rob and bully us all as he pleased.

Broken hearted, the women continued their journey. Our boys not touched, and two of our teachers being small escaped, and will be a great help as long as they can stay with the company. The Mudir said that the men had gone back to Sivas; the villagers whom we saw all declared that all those men killed. The question of what becomes of the men who are taken out of the prisons and of those who are taken from the convoy is a profound mystery. have talked with many Turks, and cannot make up my mind what to believe.

As soon as the men left us, the Turkish drivers began to rob the women, saying: "You are all going to be thrown into the Tokma Su, so you might as well give your things to us, and then we will stay by you and try to protect you." Every Turkish woman that we met said the same thing. The worst were the gendarmes, who really did more or less bad things. One of our schoolgirls was carried off by the Kurds twice, but her companions made h fuss that she brought back. I was on the run all the time from one end of the company to the other. These robbing, murdering Kurds are certainly the best-looking men have seen in this country. They steal your goods, but not everything. They do not take your bread or your stick.

As we approached the bridge over the Tokma Su, it was certainly fearful sight. As far as the eye could see over the plain was this slow-moving line of ox-carts. For hours there was not a drop of water on the road and the sun poured down its very hottest. As went on we began to see the dead from yesterday's company, and the weak began to fall by the way. The Kurds working in the fields made attacks continually, and we were half distracted. I piled as many as I could on our wagons, and pupils both boys and

Miss Graffam, Sivas 351

girls worked like heroes. One girl took baby from its dead mother and carried it until evening. Another carried a dying woman until she died. We bought water from the Kurds, not minding the beating that the boys were sure to get with it. counted forty-nine deaths but there must have been many more. One naked body of was covered with bruises. saw the Kurds robbing the bodies of those not yet entirely dead. walked, or, rather, ran, back and forth until we could see the bridge

The hills on each side were white with Kurds, who were throwing stones on the Armenians, who were slowly wending their way to the bridge. ran ahead and stood on the bridge in the midst of a crowd of Kurds, until was used up. did not see anyone thrown into the water but they said, and I believe it, that a certain Elmas, who has done handwork for me for years, was thrown over the bridge by a Kurd. Our Badvelli's wife was riding on horse with a baby in her arms, and a Kurd took hold of her to throw her over, when another Kurd said: "She has a baby in her arms, and they let her go. After crossing the bridge, we found all the Sivas people who had left before waiting by the river, as well as companies from Samsoun, Amasia and other places

The police for the first time began to interfere with me here, and it was evident that something was decided about me. The next morning after we arrived at this bridge, they wanted me to go to Malatia; but insisted that I had permission to stay with the Armenians. During the day, however, they said that the Mutessarif had ordered me to come to Malatia, and that the others were going to Kiakhta. Soon after we heard that they were going to Ourfa, there to build villages and cities. &c

In Malatia went at once to the commandant, a captain who they say has made fortune out of these exiles. told him how had gone to Erzeroum last winter, and now we pitied these women and children and wished to help them, and finally he sent me to the Mutessarif. The latter is a Kurd, apparently anxious to do the right thing; but he has been sick most of the time since he came, and the "beys" here have had things more or less their own way, and certainly horrors have been committed. I suggested that they should telegraph to Sivas and understand that had permission to go with these exiles all the way, and the answer is said to have come from Sivas that I am not to go beyond here

My friends here are very glad to have me with them, for they have a very difficult problem on their hands and are nearly crazy with the horrors they have been through here. The Mutessarif and other officials here and at Sivas have read orders from Constantinople again and again to the effect that the lives of these exiles are to be protected, and from their actions should judge that they must have received such orders; but they certainly have murdered a great many in every city. Here there were great trenches dug by the soldiers for drilling purposes. Now these trenches are all filled up, and our friends saw carts going back from the city by night. A man know told me that when he was out to inspect some work he was having done, he saw dead body which had evidently been pulled out of one of these trenches, probably by dogs. He gave word to the Government, with the result that his two servants, who were with him, were sent for by under-officers, saying that the Pasha wanted them, and they murdered. The

Beledia Reis here says that every male over ten years old is being murdered, that not one is alive, and no woman over fifteen. The truth seems to be somewhere between these two extremes.

My greatest object in going with these exiles was to help them to get started there. Many have relatives in all sorts of places, to whom I could write; and I could, in my own estimation, be a channel by which aid could get to them. I am not criticising the Government. Most of the higher officials are at their wit's end to stop these abuses and carry out the orders which they have received, but this is a flood, and it carries everything before it.

I have tried to write only what I have seen and know to be true. The reports and possibilities are very many, but the exact truth that we know, at best, calls for most earnest prayer and effort. God has come very near to many during these days.